HOW TO
NAIL

VOICE
MAIL

Profit and Prosper in Business

How to Nail Voice Mail
Profit and Prosper in Business

Shawna Schuh

Published by Schuh Biz Publications,
a subsidiary of Schuh Biz Productions,
24241 Hwy. 47, Gaston, Oregon 97119

Visit our website at: www.BusinessGraces.com

Cover design and inside layout: Ad Graphics, Inc., Tulsa, OK
Printed in the United States of America

ISBN: 0-9723193-0-1

To order additional copies of this book or to receive a
complete catalog of other products by Shawna Schuh, contact:
Schuh Biz Productions by calling toll free
877-474-2962
See the back page for an order form.

Dedication

I spent a considerable amount of time on the road with a show band in my early twenties and getting mail became my lifeline. I dedicate this book to my mother and late father, Louise and Gil Schuh, who never stopped writing and sending recorded messages when I was out there all alone. The power of mail is awesome. Thanks for using it so well!

Gratitude Is Due

Just like that story about the turtle who did not get up onto the fencepost by itself —this book would not have happened without the efforts of and encouragement from a whole slew of other folks. These pages are reality because of their helping hands and hearts.

God. The big guy is in everything and knows everything and He is the first one I thank daily. I do not believe God needs to "Nail Voice Mail" but I also know He listens and replies to "Knee Mail!"

My husband, best friend, and partner, Don Potesta. There are few things more important when writing a book, putting together a presentation, or embarking on something new than having someone who believes in you. I feel blessed to be loved by such a quality guy.

Sandy McCready, Schuh Biz Marketing. Having Sandy as an associate and friend has added a wonderful dimension and richness to my life. Sandy is one savvy lady who exemplifies courage. You are a gift from God!

Kat Cook of AD Cook & Associates. This book and a lot of the others I've written started with an idea and many of the best ideas have come out of this talented lady. Your brain and heart are powerful allies! Thanks and Love!

Girlfriends. I have a lot so I won't list them all here. Without these fabulous women who know how to use all forms of mail to communicate, I would not be the person I am. You are holding in your hands the thoughts, processes, and emotions from many generations, representing many skills. Thank you, ladies, for your support and love. And, yes, there's some "guy" energy mixed in, so thanks to you guys, too!

Contents

Introduction

Why "Nail Voice Mail?"

Welcome to this "how to" book on dealing with voice mail in these extremely stressful times.

"Stressful?" you ask? I say stressful because contrary to what we were all led to believe—that technology and the accompanying information explosion would make life easier—it has, in fact, made life more complicated. This is true for me and since you're reading this I assume it has affected your life in the same way. We have more ways to communicate than ever before, but communication remains the number one challenge for most organizations I know.

Why did I feel compelled to do a book on voice mail? Because most everyone I call or have spoken to is using it less effectively than I know they could. And, to be completely blunt, I'm tired of getting all the same old messages when I call people!

Plus as I've been working on this book and asking people how they feel about voice mail it's become quite clear that voice mail makes people emotional to say the least!

I want to share with you what I've learned about creating voice-mail messages so that you can experience the same success I've had with it. It can be a profitable business tool, if you use it well.

> *"Each man reserves to himself alone*
> *the right of being tedious."*
> **Ralph Waldo Emerson**

I know from experience that voice mail done well can make a caller's day. I know that leaving an upbeat and interesting message is refreshing and inviting. I know it helps business and builds trust. I'm here to start a voice-mail revolution!

Like your personal appearance and the visual appearance of your written communications, the impression you leave with your voice mail messages—the ones on your system and the ones you leave on others' systems—is a potent and important one. Based on the messages I hear daily, I personally think many people are still in the Stone Age. Most people I hear simply don't know how to leave an effective voice-mail impression. After reading *How to Nail Voice Mail*, you will have the tools you need to leave messages that bring joy to others and profit to you.

How to Use This Book

I've written this book in twelve chapters. Open to any page in any chapter and you are sure to learn something you can put to use immediately. My objective is to make your life easier with some new thinking about technology that is here to stay. You now have two choices. Read, agree, and do nothing—or read, agree, and get ready to "nail voice mail" so that it becomes an effective business tool rather than a pain in the neck that just adds more stress to your life!

I've included lots of voice mail examples for you to alter and use as your own. Keep this book by the phone so you'll always have ideas handy as you continue to fine-tune your messages. The ones you leave on your end are just as important as the one you leave when you get someone else's voice-mail system instead of the "real thing." If you do voice mail well anyone listening to your messages will feel like they got the real you even if not the "real thing."

Why is it important to "nail voice mail?" Because implementing the techniques in this book can help improve your relationships, which in turn will improve your life and your bottom line.

The dictionary defines **nail** in several ways including 1. An extremely slender, typically rod-shaped, rigid piece of metal. Ouch!

My favorite definition of **nail** is also listed in the Webster's Encyclopedic Unabridged Dictionary of the English Language as 4. **To say or do *exactly* the right thing; be accurate or correct.**

This second definition is the one that's in play throughout this book!

My goal for you as a reader is simple. After reading *How to Nail Voice Mail,* you will know how to get more out of the voice-mail medium, enjoy it more, and prosper more with people as a result.

This will only happen if you apply what you learn. (That's obvious, I know, but worth repeating.)

In my younger years I actually graduated from finishing school three times (a long story). However, I won't be pushing all the "correct" ways of doing things in this book. That's because my objective is to help you leave effective messages. Sometimes that has nothing to do with etiquette and everything to do with your goals. The underlying theme, though, should always be to remember that this is about *communicating with people.*

I also recommend that you review and teach others how to use the information in this book—that's the very best way to apply it. Join my revolution! The next time you are frustrated beyond belief with someone's voice mail send him or her a copy of this book as a gift. It will help you in several ways since the messages they leave will improve which is good for you and they will no doubt be appreciative that you thought so highly of them to share this vital business building tool!

I wish you well. Please feel free to e-mail, write, fax, or leave me a message. Just don't do all of those things at once! You can expect a reply and maybe even a suggestion or two—why else would I write this book, if not to help you in any and every way I can?

Peace and joy, and happy voice mailing!

Shawna Schuh

24241 Hwy. 47
Gaston, Oregon 97119
Phone: 503-662-3044
Fax: 503-662-4381
Email: Shawna@BusinessGraces.com

Chapter One

The Philosophy Behind the Voice

"The road to the heart is the ear."
Voltaire

The Blue Shirt

I was flying Delta recently on one of my many forays across the country to speak. Sitting in the airport waiting to be called for my flight I was deeply engrossed in one of my business books. When they called for frequent flyers to board, I was the only one meandering down the gangway to the plane, stuffing things in my bag and pulling out my seat assignment as I went. Later, I realized I hadn't really paid any attention to the people behind the counter since I'd gotten to the airport.

When I stepped onto the plane, a very nice flight attendant greeted me in an extremely positive manner. He practically gushed, "I'm *so* happy you're here!" I must have looked a bit surprised. I was thinking to myself, "Now this is terrific customer service!"

With that he stopped, took a good look at me, then said, "Oh, I'm sorry, you're just a passenger!"

My surprised expression did not disappear. I'm now thinking to myself, "Yes, yes I *am* a passenger—one of the reasons for this flight." But then I took a good look at him and noticed that he was wearing the exact same shirt I was—a blue one with long sleeves and a button-down collar.

"MMM," I wondered silently. "When did Delta change their uniforms? Or, when did I subconsciously begin to dress like a flight attendant?" I even had my hair pulled back in a ponytail, just like many female attendants do!

When the two of us realized what had just happened, the flight attendant and I laughed out loud. When he mentioned that they could call me if they got short-handed, I made the sign of a cross with my fingers to let him know that wasn't going to happen.

I found my seat and enjoyed a very uneventful flight. Several minutes before the landing procedures started, I headed for the back of the plane to use the facilities. I was carrying my empty cup with me and as I headed down the aisle, and made my way to the back of the plane other passengers started to hand me their garbage!

At first I was offended (for about half a second), then shrugged it off, thinking, "Why not? I'm in the service business!" I took their garbage with a smile and the other flight attendants started cheering me on from the back.

It occurred to me that day that people often don't really see *us*. Instead, they see our blue shirts. They see the image or reputation we have designed. They see the promotion or the brochure or the color, not the person behind the business.

The flight attendant's reaction taught me this important lesson first and then the passengers taught it to me again. The experience cemented the lesson that my blue shirt had better make a great impression or I won't have a very successful business.

The message you leave on your voice mail is *your* blue shirt. It's the first thing someone will hear and judge you by. Does it reflect the kind of person or business you are? The kind of service the caller will get?

> *"Be not forgetful to entertain strangers;*
> *for thereby some have entertained angels unawares."*
> **Hebrews 13:2**

After many years in business, it's pretty apparent to me that there are more wrinkled, rumpled, and unruly blue shirts around than nice crisp ones ready to serve.

Why? Because not many people think about voice mail as a vital business tool—as their crisp blue shirt or first impression. And, because *they* don't, yours will work better for you than for most *if* you make a conscious choice to make it a quality message that will get results.

Look for the Deeper Reasons

Let's start right off with the reason to leave a voice mail message on your own phone or on someone else's. If you want to add more power and punch to your voice mail, first, answer the following questions.

1. **How do I want the caller to feel when they get my voice mail message?**

2. **How do I want the listener to feel when they hear the message I've left for them?**

How do you want the caller to feel when they get your message? Answering this question is the beginning step to making your message work for you—and most people don't answer this question because they don't think to ask it of themselves.

You don't ask the question because it's not pressing. No one has ever bothered to tell you that your message is monotone or that it is just plain boring. No one has ever suggested a better way and so we do it the way we've always done it. Does this make us a bad person? Of course not, but it certainly doesn't help us in business either.

The fact is, most of us spend our time doing what is easiest—everything from the way we dress, to what we eat, to what we watch on TV. But, if you want more business, more contacts, and happier working relationships, nailing voice mail could help you reach those goals. Perfecting your messages to fit your business like a glove will help you in other areas of your business, too.

The Deepest Meaning

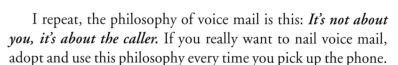

My voice mail philosophy is simply this:
It's not about you. It's about the caller.

Shawna Schuh

I repeat, the philosophy of voice mail is this: *It's not about you, it's about the caller.* If you really want to nail voice mail, adopt and use this philosophy every time you pick up the phone.

Using voice mail as a business tool has very little to do with what is easiest or simplest for you and everything to do with what is easiest and best for the caller. When we use this philosophy we are in the mode of service and respect which draws people to us.

This may seem a bit contrary because your goal in business is to do well for yourself. You need to make a profit or you won't stay in business very long, but the only way to do well for yourself is to think about how others feel when they're around you as well as the feeling they get through the phone wires. If your voice message doesn't make it easy and pleasurable for people to do business with you then maybe you're not getting all the business you'd like.

If you are just saying any old thing in the messages you leave, without really thinking about it, you're likely to get a less than satisfactory response and some callers may not leave a message at all. If they do leave a message, it may be lackluster and boring. The good news is that you can learn to use the power of this philosophy in your voice messages to get better results.

If you don't care about getting better performance from your phone, then put this book down now! If you do care, read on, knowing that your phone can't do it for it you—it's an inanimate object. Only you—in this case your voice and the content of your message—can make the difference. *Adjusting the content plus the tone, tempo, and emotion is what it takes to change a ho-hum message into one that gets results.*

The voice-mail philosophies I'm talking about make others feel special, happy, and cared for and it doesn't require a lot of work. It just takes a different approach. It means you must think before you speak into the phone. You must determine how you want people to feel when they hear your voice and your message and you must be *willing* to change some of the things you've done in the past.

So answer the first question now. *"How do I want the caller to feel when they get my voice mail message?"*

If you answered that you want a caller to:

- Feel great;
- Be ready to buy;

- Want to get to know you;
- Want to leave a message;
- Feel that you made their day;
- Feel you can help them,

then you *can* change your voice mail. You *can* leave better messages. You *can* call when it's a more effective time for both parties. If you don't want to play this way, if you think doing things the way you've always done them is fine, then expect the same results.

> *"If you mean to profit, learn to please."*
> **Winston Churchill**

So here's my offer:

Take a moment or two and decide right now:

- Do I want my callers/customers to feel valued?
- Do I want to make a great impression before someone even meets me?
- Do I want to make someone's day if I can?

If the answer to these questions is a resounding "Yes," you're ready to put this philosophy to work! The best part about doing this work, of course, is that as you make small but vital changes in the way you do your messages for your callers and listeners, *you* are the one who will benefit most. More and more people will want to be around you, call you, and do business with you. I know this is true because it works for me and for many others I know.

> *"Words are the most powerful drug*
> *used by mankind."*
> **Rudyard Kipling**

Know the Why

Let me expand on this concept. Before you do anything in life—or with your voice mail—you will profit more if you know *why* you are doing it and then figure out the best way to do it. This isn't brain surgery–it's just good common sense, which is sometimes in very short supply!

Here's a very common thought process.

- I have a phone.

- **Goal**: When I'm out, I want to know who called me so I can call them back.

- **Reason**: This could bring me more business, social activity etc.

- **Action**: Use voice mail or an answering machine.

- **Ignorance**: Be boring, lackluster, or mundane in your message, or worse yet, tell people what they already know.

- **Result**: No one feels compelled to leave a message except my mother.

- I have a phone.

Isn't this the same kind of thought process we have in many other important areas of life—everything from weight control to increasing our income? We begin somewhere, we have a general goal, and we even know the reason (even if it's broad). We take a few steps toward the goal but do not get the results we want. The reason this happens is because of the "ignorance" step. There is usually something we don't know and usually *we don't know that we don't know.*

To succeed with voice mail, use the lessons contained in this book. Apply them to your circumstances and if you find that you're not getting the results you want, continue to alter your approach in your voice messages until you do. But remember, first you need to know what you want and why it's important.

"The trick in life is to decide what's your major aim—
to be rich, a golf champion, world's best father, etc.
Once that's settled, you can get on with the happy,
orderly process of achieving it."

Stanley Goldstein

In voice mail, *always put the focus on the caller* and how you want them to feel.

New thought process:

- I have a phone.

- **Goal:** To make the caller feel good about calling whether I'm there or not.

- **Reason:** To make them feel comfortable and want to do business with me.

- **Action:** Use my voice message to make a positive impression even before the caller speaks to me in person.

- **Ignorance: None, because I've read** *How to Nail Voice Mail.* I understand it and know how to apply it to my advantage!

- **Result:** More successful interactions; people leave messages with positive comments because they get my spirit and like it. They do business with me. My bottom line improves.

- *My phone is no longer just a phone—I have a tool I know how to use to my advantage.*

"The thing that counts is not what we could do
but what we actually do."

Leo L. Spears

*   *   *   *   *

CHAPTER ONE REVIEW

1. **First impressions make lasting impressions.** Know that voice mail is your "blue shirt" and make it the best blue shirt ever. First know how you want a caller to feel. If you don't care this is not the book or knowledge for you. If you want them to feel valued you have the right philosophy.

2. **There is a thought process to everything.** For voice mail it's about Goal, Reason, Action, Knowledge, and Results.

Use the following space to write out your own goal(s), reason(s), knowledge, and the desired results for your voice messages.

Goal: _____

_____

_____

Reason: _____

_____

_____

Knowledge: _____

_____

_____

Results: _____

_____

_____

Chapter Two

Time to Tone Up!

"Those who bring sunshine to the lives of others cannot keep it from themselves."
James M. Barrie

The Good News

Here's some good news for you that whips me into a frenzy of excitement! Yes I get all excited about this topic because I love that it's so easy and works so well! Being in the entertainment industry for many years and getting to work with some high caliber people like James Gardner has shown me that we have way more control over our lives than we think. James Gardner showed me how possible it is to alter our tone and attitude for success. The truth is that we are the ones who can alter almost everything about ourselves. Isn't that a good reason to be whipped up?

When I did one of the first films I was hired for I had the great gift given to me of being in a scene with the legendary James Gardner. It was a simple scene where we establish that his character in the film is a Real Estate agent.

I was nervous but excited to meet this icon of television. I expected Maverick to come riding out on his mighty steed, or Rockford to come swinging out in his 70's garb. The assistant director told me not to attempt to shake Mr. Gardner's hand because he has arthritis and I agreed not to attempt to touch him at all. I was going to just try really hard to not gape at him.

When the assistant director called out, "Mr. Gardner is on set!" the whole set got deathly quiet and suddenly this little old, bent over man came shuffling out. My mouth was open I'm sure! I was so surprised and disappointed and thought to myself, "What am I going to tell my mother?" Other thoughts like, "This guy is the star?" and "Maybe he shouldn't have done all his own stunts." Ran through my mind.

We rehearsed the scene and he was truly lovely and such a pro. We sat together in two of those high directors' chairs and he spoke about a recent baseball game he bet money on and won. When it came time to shoot the scene we got in our places and the director yelled, "Quiet on the set!" which means they're getting ready to roll the film. I looked over at Mr. Gardner and suddenly before my eyes he started to pull himself up. He pulled up and up and shook himself straight and became magnificent right before my eyes! This time I remembered to keep my mouth closed but my eyes got bigger as I witnessed someone changing himself at will to do his job professionally and expertly.

After the shot (and he was perfect) he let himself drop down into a slouched and comfortable pose again. They say that James Gardner usually does all his scenes in one shot because he's that good. I noticed then that he wasn't really a bent over little old man, he was just an extremely humble and hardworking one that knew how to use his body and voice for success. I've never forgotten this lesson and share it often because many people say things like, "This is just the way I am!" "I've always had a high pitched voice and there's nothing I can do about it!" or even, "I can't change what God gave me!"

James Gardner proved that comments like that are pure hogwash. You *can* change your demeanor, tone, body language and circumstances *if* you want to! This is extremely good news for those wanting to nail voice mail and those wanting to be better at all aspects of their lives and business.

You are in the driver's seat! *You set the tone* of your voice-mail communication and also your success!

You also get back what you give out. If your message is upbeat and energetic, people will naturally respond to you in a similar manner. If your speech is monotone or your message sounds down, your caller will respond that way, too. If you don't believe me, try leaving a really upbeat message in place of your current one and monitor the results over a few days' time.

This concept was brought home to me recently when I went through some hard times during my dad's illness. I was tired and overwhelmed and the tone of the message I left on my voice mail was somewhat gloomy. I think it said, "Hi, You've reached the office of Shawna Schuh. I'll get back to you as soon as I can."

Now the content of my message was not bad. It stated who the caller had reached and included the promise of a call back, but you would not believe the gloomy-sounding messages I got in return. Without exception, everyone matched my tone and said something along the lines of "Call back if you want to." Or, "Shawna, I hope you're all right." How did they figure out that something was wrong with me from that simple message? The answer was loud and clear. It wasn't my message content, but rather the tone of my voice that was totally wrong. Things weren't that bad nor had I intended to imply that they were, but the gloomy tone of my voice told far more than the words.

This is a good, true-life example of the universal truth you've probably heard before: "It's not what you say but how you say it." I immediately changed the tone of my message and things improved drastically!

It's within our power to improve!

Time to Tone Up!

If you concentrate on how you want your callers to feel, you will *change your tone to one that sounds, happy, or full of energy*— or at least pleasant. Why? Because the tone of your message can be felt through the phone and that will affect your caller in either a positive or negative way.

> *"All who would win joy, must share it;*
> *happiness was born a twin."*
> **Lord Byron**

Let's face it. When someone calls you the expectation is that they will speak to you and when they reach voice mail they may be disappointed. So knowing that usually the first thought on a caller's mind is, "Oh great—voice mail!" (How irritating!) It's up to us to change that disappointment into potential.

If the message you have on your voice mail is an effective one in content and tone, you will be more likely to help that caller which is great for business. Voice mail makes some people cranky because they didn't get immediate satisfaction, so using a pleasant and upbeat tone can turn things around to your advantage by making it easier for the caller.

Knowing we can change ourselves and improve our tone and attitude is the starting point. So first you must *believe* you can tone up your message. Then there are techniques to help us to do just that and I've included them all in this book just for you!

Add a Little Love!

A Radical Thought: What would happen if you added a little love to your voice mail message?

Yes, you read that right. I said *love*. I know we're talking about something as simple and straightforward as voice mail, but you can feel love or at least warmth in someone's voice just like you can feel happiness or sadness or gloom.

> *"Anything will give up its secrets*
> *if you love it enough."*
>
> **George Washington Carver**

When I leave a voice mail message on my phone, I think about how I want my callers to feel. I make sure that my message lets them know that I appreciate their calls. The way I figure it, they've gone out of their way to pick up the phone and dial and I want to make their efforts worthwhile. With that attitude in mind, it's easy for me to add warmth and love to my voice.

There is a strong body of evidence that what we put out into the world comes back to us tenfold. This is true for voice mail as well. Think about a time when you had to deal with a small child or a baby animal—heck, even an adult animal. Did they understand your words? Of course not, but they did respond to your tone of voice—the feeling behind your words. Don't ever forget how much is conveyed through sound and feeling.

Dog gone it – it works!

I once had a mixed-breed dog named Jo. Black lab mostly but she sat low to the ground on short legs. Jo's favorite thing in the world was to be around me, that and food. Okay, she was a fatty! Besides being low to the ground she had a major problem with her hind end. She had a small delicate head and was fat from the neck down. She looked like a triangle from the back and when Jo sat down, she rolled over to one side or the other because she had no center of gravity. I really didn't over feed her—she just had low metabolism and liked to sleep most of every day.

Jo was the most loyal, loving, and adoring animal and I loved her madly despite several bad habits. One was stealing anything from any plate she could reach. If you pointed anywhere with a drumstick in your hand Jo assumed you were making her an offer—one she couldn't and didn't refuse! In addition, she often crawled under a chair to nap, only to get stuck with her ample middle in the chair legs when she got up to move. And then, there was that "other" bad habit. One winter night, when we were serving dessert to our dinner company, we had to open all the downstairs windows to continue our meal. I'm sure you get the "drift." It seemed I was always yelling at this dear pet.

One day I decided to do an experiment with Jo. As she hefted herself up to greet me when I walked in the room, I smiled and cooed to her, saying "You're an ugly dog Jo—so fat and stinky. You are a very bad dog and I hate you." Now don't get all upset and call animal control on me! I said all of these horrible things to Jo in the warmest, most pleasant tone you can imagine. She just melted on the spot, wiggling with love and attention. I laughed out loud at her reaction, especially since I used words I have *never* said to anyone—let along a dog I adored!

Then we went outside (which turned out to be a very smart move) and I changed my tone of voice on her. The minute she stepped onto the pavement, I started talking to her in a mean and menacing voice. "You're a very good dog! I love you very much! You bring me lots and lots of joy!" Jo just cowered and hung her head. But I continued, "I LOVE you SO much!" Then she acted confused and finally she went potty right in front of me—even though I had just sung her praises!

Jo showed me how important tone of voice really is. It matters, and especially on voice messages because the other person can't see your face. I'm repeating myself, but this concept is so important, it deserves repeating. In a survey I conducted while writing this book, an overwhelming number of respondents mentioned how tone of voice affected their own responses to voice messages. Here are just a few of the comments I received.

- "I can't believe how boring some people's voices are!"
- "I wish people would listen to how they sound on their voice mail and cheer it up!"
- "Sounding like you're too busy to answer your phone makes me not want to do business with you."
- "If a person comes off as insincere on their voice mail, I just forget about leaving them a message."
- "People need to remember that being pleasant is better for business than the rushed and boring messages most people have!"

Another comment that got my attention fits here with tone of voice. Respondents to my survey didn't like getting a voice message from someone's secretary, or worse yet, a computerized message. They said that practice leaves the impression that the person they called thinks of themselves as too important to answer their own calls or that they need protection from customers and clients. If this happens consistently, some callers even begin to feel like they will never get to speak to the person in charge. Besides all these unintended impressions, when you use this answering tactic, you also lose a valuable opportunity to make a positive impression with your caller through a personal message spoken in your own voice. Remember the blue shirt?

Your voice alone can speak volumes to the person on the other end of the line. So, why use another person's voice on your voice mail? Let your caller know they've reached you and that you will respond. Even if someone else screens the calls on your voice-mail system for you, leave a message in your own voice on your office line. It's a courtesy your caller deserves and will appreciate.

You Are the Tone

The truth is that people buy or need services from *people*, not from phones and not from businesses. Leaving a personal message in your own voice gets your customer or client one step closer to making the person-to-person contact that can lead to the business you want. If your message evokes warmth and appreciation, you're even closer to sealing the deal.

Don't ever forget that the tone of your voice has power. You can choose to speak in a tone that evokes any emotion you choose—love, anger, irritation, boredom, concern, or caring, to name a few. Before you record your message or leave a message for someone else, decide which tone of voice will get you what you want and use it. Just remember to be sincere. Using your own voice to get what you want is a business tool that many people simply don't think about using advantageously. While you're at it, why not try adding a little love to your tone of voice and watch what happens?

Tone-up techniques

To get you thinking about how you can "tone up" your own message, here are a few examples of "warm" messages:

- Hello! You've reached the office of Mike Dodge and I'm so glad you called! Let me know how I can help you and I will! Thanks!

- Hello! This is Bill Ford and I would love to speak with you! Please tell me the best time to return your call and I will speak with you then! Thank you!

- Hi! You've reached the office of Shawna Schuh and I'm whipped up about your call! I'll get back to you as soon as I can but have a spectacular day till then! Bye!

Speech coaches know a few tricks that you can use to warm up your message. Try these and you'll be pleasantly surprised by the results your voice messages bring your way.

Smile. When you turn the corners of your mouth up, it alters the tone that comes out. Force a smile if you have to, but turn those lips up! I have a little acronym that helps me remember to smile. You might want to copy it and put on your phone as a reminder.

S= Show
M = Magnetic
I = Infectious
L = Likable
E = Energy

"Show magnetic infectious likable energy!" How could anyone not react positively to a tone like that?

Raise the pitch. When you raise the pitch of your voice (even just a smidgen), it sounds warmer and more caring. Think about talking to an animal or child and your voice naturally raises and warms. Use the same technique when leaving a message, but take care not to sound too sweet or childlike.

Add a little air. When a person coos to a baby, they use a lot of air to send the words out. When a person is angry or irritated, the sound is clipped and more controlled. Put some air behind your words and the tone will be more pleasant. Practice cooing to your kids, spouse, animals, or the birds outside your window and you'll get the feel. Then give it a try in the next message you leave for someone.

"Out of abundance of the heart the mouth speaketh."
Matthew 12:34

*   *   *   *   *

CHAPTER TWO REVIEW

1. **Only you set the tone.** You *can* make it pleasant even when you don't feel very positive. It's a skill that can be learned. If James Gardner can do it so can you!

2. **Add a little love, or at least a little warmth.** It works wonders!

3. **Put a smile in your voice.** Show magnetic infectious likable energy and get the results you want.

4. **Raise the pitch!** Even if just a smidgen to warm up the tone and timber of your voice.

5. **Add air!** Cooing to a baby or animal is the feel and better voice mail messages are the deal! Like all great things it takes a little practice but it's worth it.

Chapter Three

Dumb Stuff

"It is so pleasant to come across people who are more stupid than ourselves. We love them at once for being so."
Jerome K. Jerome

I walked into a doctor's office the other day just before my scheduled appointment and the receptionist, someone I had never met before, asked "Are you here to see the doctor?"

I stared at her for a moment and wondered what I should say. This is what was going through my mind. "No, I just decided to walk all the way down the hall in this medical building and enter the last door on the right because I have nothing else to do with my life."

I just smiled at her and said, "Yes." I didn't say, "Hello? Isn't it obvious I'm here to see the doctor since this is a doctor's office in a medical building, or do you just think I'm so dumb that I don't know where I am on a Tuesday morning?"

I'm showing you my dark side for a moment to make a point. I'm sure the receptionist's intentions were good ones when she asked me what seemed to me to be quite obvious. However, blowing steam at a person because they unconsciously say things that

---

make you feel stupid or actually make themselves appear stupid is pretty normal for some people.

I may have helped her more by taking a light hearted approach. I could have grabbed my face in mock horror and exclaimed, "Doctor? Is this a doctor's office? I had no idea! I thought I was having a facial? Can I have a facial instead of seeing a doctor?" Instead I said, "yes" which usually gets me in less trouble!

So, what can this person do instead of asking or stating the obvious? She can *focus on the client.* Remember, when you're in a service position, just as when you're leaving a voice message, *it's all about them.* She could have greeted me with a lovely smile and asked me how I was or if there was some way in which she could help me. Or, she could have asked which doctor I was seeing that day. That would have moved us faster through the "meet-and-greet process, and I know I would have felt better served. Even if I didn't realize it, I would have been more receptive to her—a good thing since she is probably going to tell me that my doctor is running behind and I will have to wait.

The receptionist was not operating from a customer-focused philosophy when she greeted me that day. This is not surprising because most people don't operate in a customer-focused way, which is why doing so gives you such an advantage! The same thing happens all the time with voice-mail messages I hear at the other end of my phone. They aren't customer-focused.

Don't State the Obvious

When voice mail was new and people wanted to make sure you understood the medium, they left messages like the following:

"Hello, you've reached the office of Joe Motor and I'm either not here or away from the phone right now. If you'll leave your name and a message after the beep, I'll get back to you."

Duh!

Guess what? This message states the obvious, something I *already* know because I reached voice mail instead of a live voice.

If you didn't pick up and answer your phone I sorta figured out already that you were either not there or on the other line or away from the phone or unavailable or away from your desk or (need I go on?)

By now, anyone who uses a phone with any regularity knows about answering machines and voice-mail systems. They know what they are and what to do when they hear the beep—but they keep hearing messages just like the one above. Stating the obvious wastes valuable phone time that could be used to create a wonderful connection with your caller even though you're not there to physically answer the phone.

This is actually my favorite point around nailing voice mail because this type of message is so prevalent and it could be so much better. By stating the obvious on your message you waste time and give off one of the following impressions:

- You don't use creativity in your messages
- You assume the caller doesn't understand voice mail concepts

Both of the above do not help you in business. Both are mediocre ways of doing something that everyone uses but few use well.

When it comes to voice mail, people are so used to doing what they have always done that they haven't taken the time to think about how what they say might affect their callers. Guess what? If I get your voice mail, I've got a pretty good idea you're not there or you can't or don't want to answer your phone. I'd like to hear something else like when you might return calls, that you're glad I called or that you will help me.

If you're thinking to yourself right this minute, "My voice mail message says that!" this is a good place to start improving. Most everyone I know just wants to be good at what they do and help people. No one is bad for stating the obvious and in the big scheme of things it's not the most pressing issue to address. I think it is important to mention and improve because it's the little things that can make the biggest difference and stating the obvious is so mediocre but so easy to change.

If you're trying to make a caller feel good, or at least feel better, about not getting you in person then leave a better message than one that states things like:

- "I'm not at my desk"
- "I'm not here right now"
- "I'm away from the phone"
- "I'm either on the phone or away from the office"
- "I can't pick up right now"
- "I'm unavailable to take your call"

You didn't pick up the phone so we got that you couldn't!

Getting the Edge

For years, I have taught finishing and fashion concepts to people in a wide age range. My lessons have included all the niceties and social norms that make life more gracious and courteous. One of the things I shared in my classes was how to put a coat on properly—yes, there is a right way to do even this mundane task.

When I taught this technique, I would always make it very clear that putting a coat on correctly was not going to get anyone a job, make them a better person, or elevate their love life. What it *would* do was give them extra confidence. They would come across a bit more polished than most others, which could give them the edge in a hiring decision or a buying decision.

It's often the subtle things that create an emotional pull toward someone—that give him or her the edge. Haven't you met someone who made you feel at ease immediately? Someone you trusted immediately? There is something in the way a person carries themselves and the way they convey respect and confidence in their voice that is extremely subtle, but you can feel it.

Now, the good news is there are no "coat police" and there are no "voice-mail police" out there to give you a ticket for doing the wrong thing. Nonetheless, when you learn to act like there are and focus on the niceties, the underlying aura of awareness and caring that you exude has value beyond a dollar sign. People who know and do the extra things will always find their dealings with others far more successful.

Replacing the Obvious

Since we now know that we don't want to state the obvious which wastes time, makes everyone feel dumb or dumber and adds nothing positive to the experience of voice mail what do we do?

"Whenever a man does a thoroughly stupid thing, it is always from the noblest motive."
Oscar Wilde

Ask the question again. *"How do I want the caller to feel?*

- I want the caller to feel good.
- I want the caller to know that they are important to me.
- I want the caller to know I'm the right person to talk to about their needs.

Then replace the obvious statements with one or more of these.

- "I'm so glad you called!"
- "Your call is important to me."
- "If you need help with XYZ, you've reached the right place."
- "It's my pleasure to help you!"
- "You've reached the office of…"
- "I would love to return your call…"

Think about these statements. They're all pretty simple, very natural sounding, and they're all focused on the caller.

"Common sense is
the knack of seeing things as they are,
and doing things as they ought to be done."
Calvin E. Stowe

* * * * *

Chapter Three Review

1. **Stating the obvious is a waste of time for you and the caller.** Plus if you didn't pick up the phone and answer it in person the caller got very clearly that you couldn't!

2. **Subtle things are noticeable in ways that matter.** Most people won't think about your message one way or another—what they will do is feel a certain way from your message and that you have power over. Making sure you know the reason and setting the tone will produce better results.

3. **It's all about them; it's not about you.** Caller/customer focus is the best technique to use in creating a voice mail message as well as in dealing with people in person.

Chapter Four

The Sorriest Story
I Ever Heard

"A drop of honey catches more flies
than a gallon of gall."
Abraham Lincoln

How Sorry Are You?

There are some people who have discovered the very powerful purpose in apologizing. Simply put—if you are wrong, it's a great thing to do!

It's also a very difficult thing to do because admitting that you are wrong can be humbling and humiliating. On the flip side, though, it shows strong character and garners respect from those who appreciate honesty. In business, apologizing when an apology is warranted is a very big part of developing trust and royalty.

In my own experience, I've discovered that when I make a mistake and ask for forgiveness with a simple apology, I establish a better connection with my clients. Most people can relate because they've been there, too.

> *"He who never made a mistake*
> *never made a discovery."*
>
> **Samuel Smiles**

On the other hand, *apologizing is often misused* and it loses its power when it is. I'm sure you know people who preface almost everything they say with an apology, even when they haven't done anything that requires one. They're the first to say, "I'm sorry" or "I apologize for the inconvenience," often at the beginning of every conversation. The overused apology can sound very insincere and meaningless because it's used indiscriminately. The sad thing is, people who apologize all the time don't even know they're doing it or that doing so with regularity is a mode of mediocre speech that can and should be changed.

By now you probably know what I'm really talking about—the people who start their voice mail messages with an apology. Perhaps you're even saying, "OOPS! That's me!" or "What's wrong with that?"

When you begin a voice message with something like, "I'm sorry I can't take your call..." the tone of the message is already negative.

Whenever I reach a voice mail and the first thing the person says is, "I'm sorry...," I am left wondering if they will be apologizing to me throughout our relationship. (I'm also left wondering if they will end the message with "have a nice day!"—Another voice-mail phrase that has become mediocre and insincere sounding from overuse.)

When I hear "I'm sorry," at the beginning of a message it makes me want to call the next business in the phone book—one that won't be giving me negative news before I've even had a chance to talk to them.

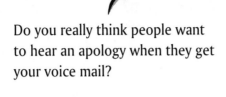

Do you really think people want
to hear an apology when they get
your voice mail?

Not everyone agrees with me on this point. For example, I was sitting in a phone sales session once and the instructor told us to always apologize for not being able to answer a call. She said something like, "Let them know you're sorry you can't help them right off the bat."

My question then and now is—"Why?"

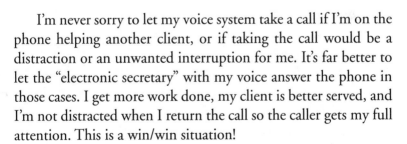

If you can't pick up the phone, you can't.

I'm never sorry to let my voice system take a call if I'm on the phone helping another client, or if taking the call would be a distraction or an unwanted interruption for me. It's far better to let the "electronic secretary" with my voice answer the phone in those cases. I get more work done, my client is better served, and I'm not distracted when I return the call so the caller gets my full attention. This is a win/win situation!

I'm not sorry and neither should you be so don't start your message in a position of apology.

Start Your Message with Power and Panache!

It may seem like the first part of this chapter is about what *not* to do—and you are absolutely right! I hope I've "nailed" home my message. *Don't apologize!*

Before you leave a message anywhere, ask yourself this key question: *How do I want the caller to feel when they hear my message? What's the most important thing I want them to do or remember?*

When you've answered this question, you are prepared to take the appropriate action to create a voice message that gets the action you want—a message that will make your callers feel better about not reaching you in person. That's called "nailing voice mail."

If you cannot begin with an apology, what should you say instead? Here are a few ideas. *Be sure to use a positive, upbeat tone of voice* (review Chapter Two for ways to do this).

- **Tell them who they have reached.** "Hi, this Shawna Schuh."

- **Tell them what to do.** For example, "Tell me when it's the best time to return your call."

If you coach your caller with the appropriate actions to take, they are more likely to leave you a positive message so you can respond in a helpful manner.

"True prosperity is the result of well-placed confidence in ourselves and our fellow man."
Benjamin Burt

It works in person, too!

By the way, this technique works just as well during face-to-face connections with people. When someone comes up to me (having never met me before) and apologizes for something, like:

- "I'm sorry, I'll be right with you."
- "Sorry for the delay."
- "I'm sorry I kept you waiting."

I don't believe the speaker is sorry. I never mind waiting—if I will get good service and I certainly don't expect an apology. Obviously, someone else was there first. I'd rather wait for undivided attention.

To change this practice into a positive—make the person waiting in line for you feel warm and wonderful instead of apologizing for doing your job. They will understand—and if not, no amount of apologizing will help anyway!

Here's how to replace the old, worn-out, insincere phrases with ones that can make a difference.

- If you usually say: "I'm sorry, I'll be right with you."
  Replace it with: "I promise I will be right with you!"

- If you usually say: "Sorry for the delay."
  Try: "How can I help you?" or "What can I do for you?

- If you usually say: "I'm sorry I kept you waiting."
  Begin with: "You have my undivided attention."

All of these phrases show that you are ready to do business with me. That's mostly what I want as a customer—not apologies!

Examples of Messages without Apologies

- "Hi! You've reached the office of Ted Buick. I'm happy you called and I promise to get back to you today by five."

- "Hello, it's March 17th and you've reached the office of Alice Honda. I'd love to help you so tell me what you need and I'll return your call."

- "Hello, this is Julie Mustang with the Road Runner Company. It's my pleasure to serve you so expect a return call soon."

- "Hi! You've reached the voice of Todd Chevrolet, which is as close to me as you'll come today. I will be returning calls on Thursday if you leave a message. Until then you can call Julie at ext. 202 for immediate service."

- "It's the voice of Buck Chrysler and I think it's great that you called. Details are ideal so leave me some and I'll get back to you soon."

Remember: Your message should leave the caller with a sense of *who you are and how you will work with them.* Be the person you say you are in your promotional materials. Offer the service your caller expects and your message will be just fine. ***Don't apologize.***

Voice mail messages should have the following components:

- Sincerity
- Warmth
- Gratitude for the call
- A promise of the action you will take

*　*　*　*　*

CHAPTER FOUR REVIEW

1. **Don't apologize** for things you cannot help or that do not require an apology.

2. **Acknowledge callers and customers positively** rather than apologetically. They just want to be helped.

3. **Make promises in your message, only if you can keep them.** People do respond more favorably to a promise, but if you don't keep your promises, they will lose faith in you.

Chapter Five

Be True to Who You Are

---

*"The best and noblest lives are those
that are set toward high ideals."*
René Alemeras

Image Is Everything

I was fortunate to be born in a rural area and unfortunate (or so I thought at the time) to be born a redhead. Stick that hair on top of pasty white skin, freckles, braces, and glasses—well, I'm sure you get the picture! Attractive? Not me. I saw myself as a gangly, unappealing country girl and I was shy and self-conscious, too. To help me gain grace and poise and, hopefully drill the tomboy out of me too, my mother signed me up for dance class, ballet to be exact. I was terrible at it.

Years later, after my share of dance classes, finishing school, make-up lessons, and theater classes, I began to emerge as a functioning female with confidence and poise—a woman who could handle herself in all social situations. This did not come easily. It came because I *was forced*. At least that's how it felt at the time.

Now, I get to thank my mother for making me take all those lessons. I get to thank all the wonderful instructors who saw past my braces and helped me shine regardless of the tinsel on my teeth!

As a professional, you probably know that people judge you by the way you look. They also consider the materials you send out, the way you speak, and your product or service part of your image. In the business world, "image is everything." It is vital, no matter how much work it takes to create a good one!

This book is concerned specifically with the image you portray in your voice mail messages—incoming *and* outgoing. Here's a key concept to keep in mind as you evaluate the efficacy of your voice mail.

> When a person or organization is doing business, it's important that the voice system is in accord with the image of the business.

Is Your Vision Blurry?

Do you have a vision statement for your business? What does it say? If the vision statement of your organization states that customers are first priority and you answer the phone like a slug, (Slimy thing found much to often in the Pacific Northwest and known to be slow and dense), then you aren't being true to your vision and your image.

I have reviewed the vision statements of many organizations over the years and not one of them ever said that the company was boring, lackluster, or uninterested in helping their clients. However I've gotten voice mail messages that screamed those very things, loud and clear.

I have received some incredibly beautiful business brochures that exuded "high end," high integrity," and "We really care about you." Unfortunately when I've called some of these companies, the person who answered the phone didn't have a clue about how to best represent the image that the organization had so carefully created in print. Was I disappointed? You bet—and I took my business elsewhere.

The same thing could be happening to you. You might be losing the contacts you need to make your business thrive, simply because your voice-mail message doesn't match the carefully groomed print image in your marketing materials. What is your voice-mail image really saying?

If you're not sure, call yourself and listen to the *tone* and the *words* you hear. If you hear your voice mail message and think to yourself, "I don't really sound like that!" It's time for a reality check. You do indeed sound like that and if you don't like it it's within your power to change it to something you and your callers will like and that fits the image and vision of your business or organization.

By the way, just like James Gardner could pick himself up and become whomever he wanted by choice—the same thing applies to all of us. This is such great news I like to remind myself (and you) often of this wondrous fact!

Practice Makes Perfect

"The voice is a second face."
Gerard Bauer

Since we get to decide what we say on our voice mail, what tone and words to use to make the greatest impact it stands to reason the image we portray is wrapped up in all of that too. All it takes is some thought, the new thinking this book is giving you and practice!

Tape yourself several times. Do it a number of different ways, changing your breath, tone, volume, level of excitement, warmth—use all the qualities of your vocal instrument. This can be very fun and you can do it on your voice mail system. Just don't forget to delete the odd ones! I usually try a couple of different things every time I change my message so that I get it the best I can. Plus sometimes I think something is really clever and then I listen back to it and think to myself, "What were you thinking?" so I put something else on there that is more in keeping with the image of who I am and what I provide to clients. This also makes me think about my image and what I do provide to my clients. It's like a mini check on my focus and if I'm being who I say I am. What a benefit!

Just Give Us You!

I just love doing business with a certain fun-loving airline because happy people answer their phones. If they must put me on hold, they play specially written music that makes me smile. I don't even mind being put on hold when I call them! It's obvious that they care about me and they've tailored their message to match their image!

The key to voice-mail image, then, is to be true to yourself and your business. If you really want to share your products and services with others, make sure your voice-mail message clearly conveys that you care about whoever is on the other end of the line.

I do not believe that any business in the world thinks of themselves as stuffy, hard to do business with or boring but that's exactly the kind of voice mail messages I hear. What's up with this?

Many people put a message on their voice mail as if it was just one more irritating thing they have to do around technology. If they act that way on their voice mail what can I expect from them in regards to service or product?

Successful people are always looking for better ways to do everything. I listen to and read the materials of the greatest thinkers of all time. All of them suggest that success comes to those that do what the average organization *isn't* doing. Doing voice mail differently from the crowd is sure to set you apart and get better results.

Please don't think I'm trying to make you do something that is uncomfortable or totally out of character for you. Just be true to who you are but take away any tone or feeling that voice mail is just another one of the many irritating parts of doing business in this current market.

If you haven't stopped yet to call your number and listen to your message, go do it now. What's your impression of you? Is it easy to reach you or do you have to go through a lot of hoops or wait through a long message before you can leave one? Do the tone of voice and the content of your message accurately convey your image in the light you think it deserves to be heard? If not get cracking on new messages right now and record them several times doing different things until you get the feel and image you want.

It's Not About Size!

Why do small operators—talking one or two person offices—(just like many of us) give long and convoluted messages? Making me go through hoops to reach one of the two people in a two-person office is a major waste of time. I hate getting a long, drawn out message that then directs me to press 1 for Bill and 2 for Sally, who just happen to be sitting side by side in their small office at the back of their home! If this scenario applies to you, please reconsider your message system. If it's set up this way just so it's easier for you to retrieve messages while you're away from the office, then it isn't set it up for your caller, but rather for yourself. *Remember, "it's all about them; it's not about you."*

The argument I've heard around this concept of all the lines and lengths is that when you have several options for callers it appears to new business that you are a going concern and can handle large amounts of business. This is supposed to leave the impression that the company is bigger than it actually is—is that being true to who you are?

I do business with companies and businesses based on the work they produce, not the size of the organization. We're living in a world where the talent you possess matters and if someone wants you and what you can provide then they want you. Your voice-mail message should make it easy to do business with you, without making your caller wait through a long message and having them press a lot of different numbers just to give them the impression you're bigger than you are.

Little Things Are Part of Bigger Things

Not too long ago I read a wonderful story in *Sidewalk Sermons* by Roy L. Smith. The "Doorknob Polishers" made the great point that there are an awful lot of people who do really great things in one small area but neglect all the other things that make a business work.

In the story, set in a shabby, run-down shop, a woman polishes the brass doorknob until it gleams. She must have it in her head that a sign of success is a bright and shiny doorknob. But when you look a little closer, you realize that the shop windows are dirty, the floor needs to be swept, and the woman herself could use a few tips on good grooming. Instead of paying attention to the total image of the shop, she is giving all of her attention to the one thing she thinks is most important.

Many of us do this constantly. We put all our efforts into the new ad or the product presentation, thinking that this will be the best use of time for our business. These things are important and cannot be neglected—but it's also important to remember some of the other things that often make an even stronger impression. What we say and how we say it when we use our voice to connect with people is one of those things that require ongoing attention.

Take some time right now to consider the entire package your present to the public, voice mail included. Is it consistent? Does it get the results you want? The good news is that if your voice mail message isn't a good match for the image you've created, it's an easy fix! Unlike your brochure or printed material or the signs you've bought and paid for! Why so many people neglect something that costs nothing and builds great impressions is why How to Nail Mail works if you use it!

> Your voice mail message is part of your image and sometimes the first or only part someone gets. Got it?

Laughing out loud

I like to laugh and have a good time. I love people and I want to serve them. I pray that everyone I deal with knows this from *every* encounter they have with me—from my written materials, to my website presence, to the message on my incoming line, to the message I leave when I reach someone else's voice mail. Because that's who I am and what my business is about so is my voice mail and it works. People often tell me, "You sound exactly like your voice mail!"

Thank you, Lord! That's the point! When I hear comments like this one, I know I'm polishing not only the doorknob but the whole package and it shines uniquely.

> Voice Mail is a tool. Sharpen it and learn how to use it to your advantage.

* * * * *

Chapter Five Review

1. Voice mail messages create images and leave an impression on your caller.

2. Use the content and tone of your voice messages to strengthen your image.

3. **Be true to who you are in your message.** Don't give a false impression of company size—focus instead on what you can do for someone!

List some traits you believe are part of your image and then post them by the phone so that when you change your message or talk with someone you're reminded about what you do and who you are. Or put your vision statement up where you can see it when using the phone—that's who you say you are!

Our business provides:

Examples	Your organization
Fun loving	
Service minded	
People focused	

Chapter Six

Extraordinary Is Just Ordinary with a Little "Extra" Added!

"He who stops being better stops being good."
Oliver Cromwell

Little Extras

I bought an ink stamp some time ago in one of those mall stores that have lots of visual appeal. I was lured in by their vast assortment of choices so I spent considerable time finding a terrific shoe design that I could use for an added bit of spirit on my business correspondence. It was an ordinary shopping experience— nothing very special. But then when the salesperson finished ringing up my small sale, she wrapped my small purchase in tissue (just like the big stores where I pay for this added perk). Then she took out a hand stamped brown paper bag with two small holes in the top and then she carefully threaded a satin ribbon through the holes and tied the bag shut with a bow. A bow on my bag! I had hardly spent a thing either but I was a customer and for the customers of this store they always do the extra. What a concept! What a great idea!

In an instant my little purchase looked like a special gift! I was charmed by this tiny and inexpensive gesture because no one had ever tied my purchase with a bow before, especially a purchase so small. Nowadays, people ask me if I even want a bag—the inference being "You'll just throw it away anyhow!" No extra, no tissue and no bow. Now, don't get me wrong. I expect great packaging from a Saks Fifth Avenue or other high-end retailer. That's part of the shopping experience and I pay for it. But this small retailer won me over with a simple, out-of-the-ordinary gesture. I'm sure this small gesture has something to do with the fact that I now own more rubber stamps than I will ever use—and I'm happy as can be about it!

When I was first studying human potential and got my hands on all kinds of books of success and accomplishment I read something that has never left me. It was the difference between ordinary and extraordinary. There is only a little difference in the spelling—just adding the word extra and viola! You have such a different word it's amazing. The word ordinary is just that—same, expected, boring, bland, what the normal do and the line that separates the good from the bad. When something is ordinary it isn't special, it isn't outstanding it just is—ordinary.

But with just a little extra—you have a whole new view of the world. Extraordinary is exceptional, special, unique and different. People are drawn to extraordinary and they want to know people who are extraordinary and have something added.

We can be extraordinary in lots of things especially our voice mail which then leads people to want to do business with us. The bow is what made that store extraordinary and the thing that brought me back many times. Okay, it wasn't the bow; it was the simple but profound fact that they did that extra thing for everyone no matter the cost of the purchase. I believe they wanted their customers to feel special and good and positive. We can do the same thing with our voice mail and all parts of our business and those who do the extras seem to do the best.

Be Extraordinary

The concept: Giving a little unexpected extra *turns ordinary into extraordinary*. Because it works and because it feels great to do it, doing something extra has become my style. I like to give gifts, offer to help out when I can, and brighten someone's day. Giving a little extra on my voice mail is a no brainer to me because it's easy to do and works. I usually include a short thought or a funny tidbit in my voice mail so that anyone calling gets a little something extra from me that day.

One note of caution when adding something extra to your voice mail—people can be easily offended (which is really too bad). So you need to ask yourself why you are adding something extra and if you are doing it to make someone smile, make them think or question it's a good thing. To make someone feel good is reason enough for me. When people feel good they do good. Productivity improves, business improves, and life is sweet!

> *"To enjoy and give enjoyment, without injury to yourself or others; this is true morality."*
> **Nicolas Chamfort**

Careful also of messages that are much too cheery or contrived, these also turn most people off. If you are not the kind of person to add something humorous to your voice mail message then leave it off. The rule is simple. If you don't feel comfortable saying it, *don't*! Always ask yourself whether what you're planning to say on your message will make your callers feel the way you want them to feel about you and your business.

I get lots of compliments from callers on my voice messages and thank yous for brightening their day. Some people have told me they've even had friends or associates call me just so they can listen to my message! Now that's what I like to hear! Many people who have put my technique to the test report that they are also getting positive feedback on their new voice mail messages.

Hmmm. If people are telling other people to call and they are, could this lead to more business? Could it also lead to a better reputation and more memorable encounters with clients? Yes indeed it works! Adding something extra accomplishes my goal—to leave a memorable impression of someone who approaches business with a smile or a helping hand.

Keep It Simple

If this fits your style, it's an easy thing to add something extra to your message. To get started, look for a book of inspirational quotes or upbeat humor and choose something that you like and feel comfortable repeating.

"He that sows thistles shall reap prickles."

Here are the criteria I use when I want to add something "extra" to my voice mail message.

The bit or quote needs to be:

- Short; people are busy.
- Enriching; it should lift the caller's spirits by eliciting a smile or provoking thought.

Here are a few bits I use; feel free to try them or find others that you like better…

- A bird in the hand is safer than one overhead!
- An idea is a curious thing—it will not work unless you do.
- Laughter is a tranquilizer with no side effects.
- Truce is better than friction.
- Did you know the Ten Commandments are not multiple choice?
- Age is not important unless you're a cheese.
- If it goes without saying—let it.
- Why not go out on the limb? That's where all the fruit is.

Please note that each of these is a short sentence and each one has a lesson or provokes thought.

What About Using Celebrity Voices?

Using a celebrity or a celebrity knock-off voice on your voice mail will only work if it fits you and the image of your business. Always go back to the main goal: How do I want my callers to feel when they get my message? Use someone else's voice *only if it fits the image* you want to portray for your business or organization.

Let's suppose you're a talent agency with lots of great character voices to promote. It would make good sense to feature one or more of them on your voice-mail messages to show potential clients that you have the voice talents they need. Bookings could result from this business voice-mail tactic. In other words, if you don't operate a talent agency, using the voice of Fred Flintstone is probably not a good idea…Yabba Dabba Do!

*   *   *   *   *

Chapter Six Review

1. **Get a book of quotes and do some exploring.** I love to spend time in a quote book and I own several. One I looked in just for this review page was, The Quotable Woman from Running Press and the quote I stumbled upon which I liked right now was this,

"If you are all wrapped up in yourself,
you are overdressed."

Kate Halverson

Another one or two that gave me pause for thought:

"It is hard to fight an enemy who
has outposts in your head."

Sally Kempton

"If truth is beauty, how come no one has
their hair done in a library?

Lily Tomlin

2. **Decide on something extra you can add to your voice mail for added interest and pizzazz.** Simply adding a smile or warmth to your tone of voice is a great place to start.

3. **Keep whatever you add to your message short and to the point.**

4. **Make your message stand out from the crowd.** Do something even a little bit different on your voice message, and yours is bound to stand out from the crowd of average or mediocre messages that people hear everyday. Remember doing the ordinary is normal and doing the "extra" really makes things extraordinary!

Midway Voice Mail Review

Let's go over the points we've covered so far since I am of the strong opinion that repetition is imperative to retention—I mean why do we go to church when we know the stories if not to be reminded?

Ask yourself:

- "How do I want the caller or customer to feel?"
- "What image am I showing with my tone, message, and manner?"
- "Am I stating the obvious?"
- "Am I apologizing for something I can't help? If so why?"
- "Have I given a little extra with my voice and/or in the message?"
- "If I called this number or got this message, would I feel compelled to leave a message or do business with this person?"

"He who succeeds makes an important thing
of the immediate task."
William Feather

Chapter Seven

Out of Town but Not Out of Mind!

"Travel: Some good advice
From one who knows:
Take twice the cash
And half the clothes."
Anonymous

Promises, Promises

The other morning I was listening to a disc jockey going on and on about his recent vacation—how great it was to get away, etc., etc. He also did a call-in survey, asking for responses to this question: "What do 57% of the people do on their vacations?" Well, I just love a quiz—my mind was racing with possible answers! What do most people do on vacation? Swim? Go to an amusement park? Read? Sleep? What do I always do on vacation? When was the last time I took a vacation? But, I digress.

The very first caller got it right when she said, "Call in to work!"

I shook my head in wonder at my complete lack of thinking skills. Of course they call work! Don't I always check my messages after being away for a day or two just to make sure my clients are fine, that someone doesn't need something only I can provide, and to see how sales are going? I guess I'm not alone there!

> *"Traveling is one way of lengthening life,*
> *at least in appearance."*
> **Benjamin Franklin**

I am not about to judge this practice and I do believe time away is essential for increased productivity, but if you have promised to check your voice mail while you are away, be sure you keep that promise!

A promise is a promise. If the message you leave on your voice mail while you are away makes a promise to check your messages or return calls within a certain time, make sure you keep that promise or don't make it!

If you don't intend to check in when you are off on some enchanted island, then don't say you will. Instead, I believe it's vital to be honest and let your callers know that you will be unavailable for the day or the next week, or whatever. If possible, give them the option of speaking to someone else in your organization who can help them while you are away. If you don't employ this courtesy, your callers will have no idea why you haven't returned their calls. That leads to frustration and concern that perhaps you didn't get their message—or worse yet, that you don't care enough about them to return their call! That's not the message you want to send!

If you are away from your office, or can't return calls even though you are there, your message should include the following information:

• When you will return their calls
• Other possible options for assistance— if available

The Courtesy of a Call Back

Let's address the courtesy of a call back. How often have you gotten a voice-mail message that says "I am in the office today," but your call was never returned? Doesn't it make you wonder why you don't rate a return call? If you are in the office, but you're not answering your phone, don't leave a message that says you're there. Instead, let me know when you will be returning messages so I'm not left hanging all day wondering if you got my call. Better still, if you need a day in the office without interruptions, refer me to someone else if possible. If you are out of the office for an extended period of time, let me know that, too, so I can get satisfaction somewhere else if possible.

Simply stating that you are out of the office until Tuesday of next week isn't of much value to your caller, especially if they really need assistance when they call. Always remember that your focus should be on the caller, so include something in your message that helps them solve the problem or get the information they need—or at least let them know when you will be able to help them with a return call.

"Magnificent promises are always to be suspected."
Theodore W. Parker

I'm not a fan of giving the exact date of return...

If you say you are going to be back in the office Monday the 17th and will return calls that day, then you'd better be prepared to spend the day doing it. Remember that you promised so now you're in a corner to return those calls even if something else that needs your attention comes up. Better to state that you will be back the week of the 17th and will return calls as soon as possible.

And don't forget to change your message on Monday the 17th! We've all gotten messages that say we'll be gone until a certain time and the message is still there three days after the return date. Sloppy way to do business don't you think?

Are You Ready to Receive?

When you do take the time to listen to your voice messages, make sure you are ready to receive them. Responding to voice mail after a day or a week or a month away won't be a tedious chore if you are prepared and set a time limit.

Be prepared

- **Have a pad and pen handy so you get those messages down.** I keep a small notebook in my bag for this express purpose. That way, everything gets recorded in one place rather than on the back of a business card or a stray scrap of paper. I put the information I need down, the name of the caller and number and then I make myself a note to refer back to.

- **Delete the message only after you have written down all the pertinent information.** (Callers hate hearing, "So-and-so's voice mail is full.")
- **Take the appropriate action for each message and check it off.**

In my office, I keep a 6" x 8.5" three-ring binder for retrieving messages. It's a thick one so there's plenty of room for recording messages plus any notes to myself that are appropriate. I keep it in a special stand right by the phone so it's always there when I need it. That way I have a record of my calls. I often refer to it when I need to go back and retrieve someone's phone number.

I also make a habit of reviewing and removing pages that no longer require action so it's easy to locate what I do need. Using the notebook faithfully and referring to it often eliminates the necessity of replaying messages and helps me remember to follow through on a message when necessary.

When I return a call, but get a voice message, I code that call in my notebook with an "M," indicating that I've left a message in response. If I reach the person I'm calling or resolve the issue in some other satisfactory way (referring it elsewhere, for example), I cross it out. Sometimes leaving a message for the caller is all that is required—reaching them in person is often not necessary if the message I received is clear about what they need from me.

Set a time limit

Allow a set amount of time to answer voice mail messages and stop when you reach that time limit. I keep a timer on my desk and use it often. Responding to them will be faster and more efficient if you've recorded all the necessary information first and located any information or resources you need to answer your callers' needs. The timer reminds me to take care of business and to keep small talk to a minimum. Returning your voice-mail messages is vital to your business. Handling it in a timely manner is essential.

Examples of Out-of-Office Voice Messages

- "Hi! You've reached the office of Joe Bronco. I'm out of the office until Friday but will be checking in and will get back to you as soon as I have a break—but remember that time is the most valuable thing a person can spend."

- "Hi! This is Jim Sable. I'm attending a conference all week, but I will check my messages at 10 AM and 3 PM each day. If you tell me what you need, I will return your call within a half-hour of those times within the following three days."

- "Hello, you've reached Don Colt and I'd love to help you. If you need immediate assistance, call my associate Julie Beetle at 000-0000, or leave me a message. When I return, I will get back to you within 24 hours."

All of the examples below follow the *How to Nail Voice Mail* rules because they:

- Make the caller feel good;
- Have an upbeat tone;
- Include helpful information;
- Are short and to the point;
- Include the desired action for the caller to take;
- One includes an extra quote!

It's important to note that each of the above examples also includes a promise.

If you don't intend to or cannot keep a promise, don't include one in your message.

"A promise is an I.O.U."
Robert Half

My travel schedule for presentations is often quite hectic (and I'm often frantic) so I never promise to return calls at a specific time. I prefer not to make a promise that I might not be able to keep, causing a disappointed or dissatisfied customer.

I do, however, state that I *will get back to them* and I *always* keep that promise. I want all callers to have a satisfying experience when they cannot reach me in person so that they also make the assumption that their personal experience with me will be more than satisfactory. That's simply being true to who I am as a service provider.

Urgency – or Emergency?

It's important to distinguish between leaving messages that spell out emergencies or urgencies and ones that may be important. I know a woman who always states on her voice mail message, "If this is an emergency please press 2 for assistance." Unless you are a doctor's office or hospital most things are not an emergency so very few people will press 2 and some won't even leave a message. She is inadvertently giving the impression that she only wants to hear from those who need something now. Businesses survive on serving customers even if the current need is less than profitable knowing full well that profits come from people who feel served. Let me repeat that:

Businesses survive on serving customers—even if the current customer need is less than profitable now—knowing full well that profits come from people who feel served. Les Schwab is a prime example of this philosophy. Les Schwab is a tire store in the Oregon area and they will fix your flat and charge you nothing but say, "Next time you need new tires think of us" and people do. My husband wouldn't go anywhere else but Les Schwab because they helped him once when he was in desperate need and never charged him a cent—so now he's spent hundreds (probably thousands) of dollars with this company.

A lot of people want immediate assistance because they may be calling to get general information. Like to get a price on a product you sell or want to know how late you are open. These people won't leave a message because they may figure they won't get the information in a timely manner so they hang up and call the next business in the phone book. I know I always hang up on a general communication when I want some real information like how much it costs to clean a carpet or get the windows cleaned.

So how do you get people to leave a message or want to call back when you have a service business and you're away from the phone a lot? By leaving compelling messages that callers are drawn to. By stating a promise so they know what to expect or by giving them options. If you don't want callers to leave messages use words that scare them like, emergency, urgent or important. The number of calls most businesses get that fall into these categories is slim. Why not be more open and warm so that people want to do business with you?

Webster's Dictionary defines **emergency** as: a sudden, urgent, usually unforeseen occurrence or occasion requiring *immediate* action.

Immediate is the key word here. We usually associate this with the need to dial 9-1-1 for assistance.

Webster's defines **urgent** as: pressing, compelling, or requiring immediate action or attention; imperative. Urgency is often expressed with insistence, as requests or appeals in an *urgent* tone of voice.

What should you say instead? Here are a few examples.

- "You've reached the voice mail of Lester Lincoln. I will be unable to answer calls today, so please call 000-0000 to get help today. Our goal is to serve you!

- "Hello! You've reached the office of Harry Honda and I would love to help you! I will return to the office tomorrow at 10 AM, but if you need something now, press 0 for an operator. Thanks for your call!"

- "Hi! This is the voice of Mitch Mazda. I'm out of the office all week but I *am* checking messages. We want to help you so please let me know what you need and I promise some answers for you even if someone else returns your call. Be well!"

All of the above messages follow the *How to Nail Voice Mail* rules, plus they offer the promise that all calls are important and deserve attention as soon as possible.

Give your caller one of three options when you cannot take their call:

- Who to call to get service now;

- An extension number to press for service (the easiest one for the caller, if it's available through your system);

- The promise of a call back from someone else if they let you know what they need in their message.

Avoid Too Much Information

A voice message that goes on and on, sharing more information than is necessary or important to the caller is irritating to say the least.

In the survey I did for this book going on and on in voice mail was mentioned often and not in a complementary way. Before you leave a message to cover you while you are away from the office, remember that the caller cares less about where you are and what you will be doing than about getting the information or service they need or want as soon as possible. Here's an example of a less-than-helpful message:

"Hi! You've reached the voice mail of Rod Rambler and I'm in Hawaii visiting my oldest daughter, Louise, for the birth of her first child. That's right! I'm a grandfather now! It's a boy and they say he looks just like me! I'll return to the office on February 17th, but until then I'm soaking up the sun and having fun! Talk to you soon! Bye!"

Sometimes a message like this rambles on with even more unnecessary information such as "leave your name and message at the beep and I will return your call and don't forget to speak slowly!" Although this message might be appropriate on a home phone that does not take business calls, it's not so good if you are a professional. It's simply too long and far too personal though we're all happy about the new bundle of joy!

Here's another example of too much sharing:

"Hello you've reached Julie at extension 437 in the HR Department and I'm conducting training on Wednesday, Thursday, and Friday of this week so it will be very difficult to return your call. Next week I'm only training on Tuesday, so if you'll leave me a detailed message I may be able to get back to you on Monday or Wednesday of next week. If those days don't work for you, then I can get back to you later in the week but I'm going into additional training the week after so I'll get back to you as soon as I can. It's a busy time here so please understand and thanks for your call."

This message from Julie is *not* tailored to the caller, but rather goes on and on about *her* hectic pace. I get the feeling that even if I did try to reach her at the times specified in the message, she wouldn't be able to help me.

> Avoid sharing information about how busy you are or how little time you have. You may think it sounds like you are in demand and highly successful, but it can also send a negative message—one that says you are very disorganized or that you can't handle your busy schedule.

Remember, to "nail voice mail," you must *always focus on your caller and how you want them to feel. It's not about you!* Both examples cited above are about the person leaving the message, not about the caller/customer.

Voice mail is a business tool and if you remember that the tool is for you to use to your callers' advantage and ultimately your own, you will eliminate some of the more irritating aspects of this technology.

If you've gotten this far and taken appropriate action based on what you've learned, you have already altered your current message by changing your tone of voice, adding a smile, and letting callers know that even when you're not in your office, you're always in touch and you value their calls.

"We work not only to produce but to give value to time."
Eugene Delacroix

*　*　*　*　*

Chapter Seven Review

1. **Let callers know how long you will be away**—a day, a week, a month, whatever.

2. **Be prepared to take down accurate information** when you call in for messages so you can return calls with accuracy and efficiency.

3. **Don't make a promise in your message unless you can keep it.**

4. **Don't share unimportant or overly personal information** in your message.

5. **Focus the message on meeting the needs of the caller.**

Chapter Eight

The Caller Is King!

*"It is always with the best intentions
that the worst work is done."*
Oscar Wilde

There was a story I read from a journalist who was reviewing some of the best lessons he had learned in his long and distinguished career. I read the article years ago, don't know the name of the author but the story stayed with me. And even though I may have changed much of the details—the lesson I learned is still very clear.

It seems when this journalist was young and fresh out of school he got a low-level position at a large paper. He was assigned to interview a king of a small country that was visiting the United States. This was his first assignment and he was feeling unsure about himself. Not because he didn't believe in his skill as a reporter, but because he was young and not well versed in social skills and eating with royalty. The king and he were to have lunch at the splendid hotel where the king was staying while in the city.

When he arrived at the door of the hotel room where the king was staying he expected to see a wait staff person, or assistant but the king answered the door himself. The king took the reporter's coat and seated him. He poured the beverages and when the lunch tray came, the king did the serving of lunch himself. They had a wonderful time. The reporter was at ease, felt like he really got to know the king and also felt that even though he didn't know the social rules hadn't made any mistakes during the lunch or meeting.

After the interview the young reporter went back to the paper and wrote a truly engaging article that got lots of recognition. The king sent a fantastic recommendation letter and kept in contact with the reporter and his career blossomed.

As the reporter grew older and became a lot more wise he started to recognize the things he was poor at, those social skills he lacked and all of the mistakes he had made while dining with the king those many years ago.

As I was reading his story his point became very clear that in hindsight he realized that he had made many mistakes the day he dined with a king. From the improper use of utensils, to how familiar he was with royalty in the way he addressed the king. And even in the questions he asked. After thinking about it the journalist came to this conclusion. For every mistake that he had made, the king had also made the same mistake. Every time the journalist used the wrong utensil, the king used the wrong one too. The King modeled the journalist's behavior and put him at ease. Because the King focused on the young journalist the young man felt special and comfortable in what might have been a very uncomfortable situation.

Wow! My take is strong that the king was not only very gracious and kind but one very smart cookie! (I wonder how he would feel about being called a cookie? Probably fine since this is one savvy king!)

The king knew the rules; he had been practicing social and professional etiquette for his entire life. But he suspended the rules to make someone else feel comfortable and welcome.

> You can't rule people with rules.
> You serve people with love.

This is astounding stuff when you think about how well this can serve you in business. The whole philosophy of How to Nail Voice Mail is about putting the caller first. Doing a bit more than normal for huge benefit. But the rub is this; you can't suspend the rules until you know the rules. You can't use voice mail to advantage until you understand the philosophy of why it works and learn that this tiny tool holds huge potential.

Following are some very common mistakes people make with their phones. Read with the king's perspective—how do I want the caller/customer to feel?

"The greatest revolution of our generation is the discovery that human beings, by changing the inner attitudes of their minds, can change the outer aspects of their lives."

William James

Clean up the Screening

If you have a system that lets you screen calls, caller ID etc. that's a great benefit to you but not any benefit to your callers except that if you aren't in the mood to give great service you won't pick up the phone. These services are terrific to keep you up and engaging for your callers but if you use them don't give yourself away and pick up during a message. Picking up while someone is leaving you a message immediately alerts the person calling that you screen calls and can make you look unprofessional.

When you pick up on the message the caller is caught off base, which puts them in an uncomfortable position and possibly makes them repeat what they've already said. Making them feel stupid or flustered. Is that your goal? Plus, you instill in their minds that you screen calls and that will make this caller suspicious the next time they call and you don't pick up. Don't set yourself up for trouble. Don't pick up during a message. Yes this sounds like I think people are suspicious which is not the truth. I think people are wonderful—but I've felt odd when someone answers knowing it's me and I'm not the suspicious type so imagine how suspicious people feel when you pick up in the middle of the message one time and not the next?

One exception to the rule

If you have the kind of system that lets you listen - and you just get into the office and want to grab the phone go ahead. That person will know you just got in by your demeanor and out of breath tone and won't feel anything but grateful that they got you. Except of course if they have to then repeat everything they just said on the voice mail!

In the case of caller ID

I have a very good friend who always picks up by saying, "Shawna—so great to talk with you!" or "Shawna—how are you?" She always makes me feel very warm and loved but for some strange reason I also have it in the back of my mind that on a day she didn't want to speak to me I wouldn't get her at all which is the whole reason to have caller ID! Which is the point—caller ID is for the person who has it and is not a benefit to the caller so there is no reason to let your callers know you use it. The beauty of technology is that we can use it to our benefit and it doesn't matter to a caller one way or another if you use it if they get good service when they call.

I strongly believe you shouldn't pick up the phone at all if you are not in a mood to serve the person on the other line.

When you answer the phone by stating the callers name before they've even said hello your caller knows they have been screened (and made it this time) which puts you at the advantage and the caller at the disadvantage in their mind. You still have the advantage when using caller ID but you don't need to let me know you have it. This goes right back to our original goal of: How do I want the caller to feel?

Make it easy on yourself and use caller ID or screening all you want—just don't let your caller in on it! Just answer the phone the way you always do—warm, engaging and glad for the call and you will make your callers/customers feel terrific and more ready to buy!

"The measure of a man's real character is what he would do if he knew he would never be found out."
Thomas B. Macaulay

The Number Mummer

Ever get a message that repeats the number you just called? What should someone feel like after they've heard, "You've reached, 555-5555 please leave a message." Here's what I feel like, "I know I've reached 555-5555 that's the number I called! Do you think I can't count?" Or: "Is that the number I called?" I better check! So I scramble around on my desk to check the number because as soon as it's dialed out of the mind it flew!

I believe that when someone leaves the number that was just called on their voice mail they were trying to help the caller. (I would hope so or why do it?) I would assume that they think that by repeating the number that was just called they are helping the caller determine if they got it right. But seriously, after I've dialed a number I don't remember what the exact numbers were and I would much prefer to be told the name of the party I reached instead of a repeat of numbers I don't care about. Plus it seems like a waste of recording time.

If I hear this message, "Hi! You've reached Donna & Bill..." and I did not intend to call someone named Donna and Bill I can hang up before I waste anymore of their or my time. But when they leave the number 555-5555 I have to stop and think, "Was that the number I called?" or I have to hope I dialed right and leave a message for whoever is living at 555-5555. This is a cumbersome way to go about things. First, it forces the caller to try to remember the number they just called, or frantically look in their book to see. Second, it doesn't mean anything to the caller. Third, it doesn't leave a good impression of the person being called. A better solution is to state your name or tell the caller you're glad they called.

Examples of more good messages:

"Hi! You've reached Ted & Alice and we can call you back later if you like! The beeps are long and the time is short! Talk with you soon!"

"Hello, you've reached the office of Ted Tercel in accounting. I'll punch your numbers as soon as I return! Thanks for your call!"

"It's the voice of Alice Acura here to let you know I will return your call promptly! Thank you for calling and we can't wait to serve you!"

All of these are short, simple and give the caller a flavor of the person's personality. Nailing voice mail is simple if you think about what you are trying to accomplish and follow the example of the King!

> *"Life is only this place, this time,*
> *and these people right here and now!"*
> **Vincent Collins**

*　　*　　*　　*　　*

Chapter Eight Review

1. **Treat all people special.** Even if you know more rules or social skills it's best to make another feel special than yourself right.

2. **Don't answer when you can't give the caller your attention.** When you think of the phone as a business tool and not an alarm you'll only answer the phone when you can serve the person who is calling.

3. **Screening calls and using caller ID is for the benefit of you.** Your callers don't need to know you use these services since it doesn't benefit them.

4. **Repeating the number just called wastes time**—the name is the most important thing to most people. Use yours and theirs.

Chapter Nine

Common Sense Is Not So Common!

"Common sense in an uncommon degree is what the world calls wisdom."
Samuel Taylor Coleridge

Don't Pick Up That Phone!

Writing a book is quite an undertaking and it takes some dedicated time and discipline to get it done. When I was working on the book you are now holding in your hands I would set aside some writing time and try to stick to my schedule. Then the phone would ring and my hand would start to reach for it because it seems to be shouting at me, "Pick me up! Pick me up!" and it's so hard to ignore that insistent sound. If I went with my impulse and answered the phone (maybe not in my merriest voice) and got a nuisance call I was sorry and I'm sure my tone reflected it. I consider nuisance calls those calls from a family member who just wants to check in, a telemarketer who wants to bend my ear or someone who called me by mistake. I'm now out of my flow, a tiny bit irritated (with myself mostly) and it takes me additional time to get back into my project. Plus no one got served. So if you're really involved in a task or a project and answering the phone would be an unwanted interference or nuisance, ***don't answer it!*** It's just that simple.

> Answer the phone only when you are ready to give the caller the undivided attention they deserve.

When NOT to Answer Your Phone

You're with a customer. Nothing irks me more when I'm working with someone who can't resist his or her ringing phone. That is downright discourteous to me—and to their caller. If I've gone out of my way to arrange to meet with you, I deserve your undivided attention. I feel unimportant and disregarded if the phone is more important than my presence.

I can just hear you say, "But I might lose some business if I don't answer." That could be true, but if you pick up a call while you're in an active appointment with someone else, you could lose that business or make a really bad impression. Even if I do buy something or enlist your services that day because I'm there, answering your phone could cost you my loyalty and respect. If you are with me, then please be with me 100%.

You've scheduled a set time to work on a project. When you have set a goal, don't treat your ringing phone like it is an emergency. Check your messages after you have completed what you set out to do during a specified time period. Your callers are bound to get a better response from you because you can focus on them when you do return their calls—and because you feel good about what you've just accomplished.

You are in a meeting. Taking calls during a meeting is downright rude. Of course, there could be an exception to this—your wife is giving birth or there is a real medical emergency that needs your attention. Other meeting attendees are certain to understand in special cases. Otherwise, they deserve your undivided respect and attention. If there is an important call coming in and you know it, alert those in the meeting ahead of time that you must take it; that gives them the opportunity to be accepting instead of insulted. Otherwise, turn the cell phone off or put your office phone in the answering mode before the meeting begins.

You are in a foul mood. Don't pick up the phone if you have a bad attitude or something has just upset you. Your tone of voice will give you away for sure. In this case, it's better to let your message system take over or have someone else answer your calls temporarily. Bad moods are easy to get into and spread like wild fire so take some time to cool off, count your blessings or have a stiff drink but don't answer the phone!

Something that always helps raise my spirits is thinking of the phone ringing as the sound of a cash register. That "cha-ching, cha-ching" is music to my ears. It makes me smile every time!

Plan for Success

Many successful people who receive and make a lot of phone calls, set aside a certain time each day to take care of this task. This is a very wise strategy. When you purposely schedule time to pick up voice messages and to return calls, you can get your mind in the right attitude and warm up your voice so you are the pleasant, professional person your callers expect and deserve. If this is an appointment you make with yourself everyday; it allows you to let your callers know when they can expect to hear back from you. That could increase the likelihood that they will be available when you call. This habit is really using your common sense, something that isn't commonly used enough when it comes to utilizing voice mail.

Don't Blame Me!

I called someone the other day—someone I didn't know—about a service they offer. It was an inquiry. This type of call often leads to new business for me so it could lead to new business for this person. This is the message I heard:

> "You've reached Jim Ferrari, I'm not here right now but if you'll leave your name and number S-L-O-W-L-Y after the beep I'll get back to you but only if you go S-L-O-W!"

Obviously, Jim has had a difficult time in the past with callers who rushed their information and he didn't get it. He probably had to listen to the message several times to get the right information—or perhaps he couldn't decipher it at all. He probably thinks he's lost business because the caller was in a hurry, was inconsiderate, or doesn't understand the concept of voice mail as a business tool.

You know what? Jim's message indicated to me that he doesn't understand the concept of voice mail as a business tool either. When I hear this kind of message, I might feel chastised right off the bat for speaking too fast or get the idea that you think I can't leave a clear message. Some quick thinker who gets Jim's message might leave this kind of message in response:

"Hi Jim, I'll go really s-l-o-w for you so you can get the number. 5-5-5—5-5-5-5. Is that s-l-o-w enough for you Jim?"

Jim might get a kick out of this response, or he just might be irritated because the messages he retrieves in response to his are too long when everyone speaks slowly—at his request! Some people (I'm one of them) might not leave a message at all. You can learn a valuable lesson from this example.

Voice mail shouldn't be used to chastise your callers or tell them how to speak.

Don't Try to Educate Me Either!

It is not your job to use your voice message to educate the rest of the world about how to use voice mail. That's the job of this book! Your mission is to leave the impression that your caller will want to work with you. You can do a lot for voice mail in general, simply by using your own message effectively to set a good example for others. Here are some examples of voice messages that are too "teachy" or overly demanding:

- "Please leave your number twice!"

- "Please speak very slowly!"

- "Tell me the time and date you called."

- "Leave your name and phone number and any important information."

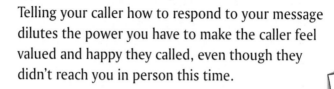

Telling your caller how to respond to your message dilutes the power you have to make the caller feel valued and happy they called, even though they didn't reach you in person this time.

Yes, you will get many messages that you consider less than satisfactory or uninteresting; however, *your* messages will set you apart from the crowd because you know how to leave an effective and interesting message. You will do it right!

"They know enough who know how to learn."

Henry Adams

Don't Tell Me Your Problems!

Have you ever gotten messages like these?

- "I'm here today but in meetings all afternoon."
- "I need you to be concise since I have limited time during this final quarter."
- "I will be in training all day but leave a message anyway."
- "I'll be in Nashville then on to Knoxville and finally Clarksville so leave me a message and I'll try to return your call."

These messages all focus on you, not on your caller. The bottom line is your caller really doesn't care where you are, what you're doing, or how busy you are. Your caller wants you to get the message and get a response that meets their needs, as soon as possible!

When I get this type of answer, I often think to myself, "Well, I might as well call the *next* business in the Yellow Pages. I won't be hearing back from this one any time soon." It's easy to make these message more caller- friendly. Simply change the focus from self-serving to caller serving.

Let's look at ways in which the previous messages could be re-focused on the caller.

"I'm here today but in meetings all afternoon." When you say something like this, you are teasing me since I can't talk to you. You are there but I can't reach you—I missed you by a nose. This makes me feel like a failure—in a very subtle way. In addition, I don't need to know that you are in meetings all day—that information is of no use to me and it's a waste of message space. Plus in the purest form if I've called you after hours or at midnight you probably aren't there or in a meeting currently.

So what message can I leave if I'm going to be in meetings all day? Here's a good example:

"Hello, you've reached the office of Nancy Cadillac and I'm glad you called! I am not able to help you personally today but you can get information and answers by pushing 0. If you want me to return your call in person, I will when I return to the office. Thank you for your time!"

Another:

"Hi, You've reached the office of Albert Austin and I will return your call when I'm back in the office which will be tomorrow the 25th. Thank you and if you can't wait that long press 0 for another service associate."

"I need you to be concise since I have limited time during this final quarter." This one makes the person who placed the message seem so busy and important that the caller might feel less so. The information is of no use to the caller and has a demanding tone (be concise).

Here's a better message:

"Hello! This is Rhoda Hummer and I would love to speak with you! Please let me know your needs and how I can help you so when I return your call I'm prepared for you! Have a wonderful day and thank you for calling!"

Another:

"Hi, this is Julie Sting Ray and you're no doubt as busy as I am so let's help each other! I'll return your call with whatever information you need in the next two days. If you would like to speak to me in person a time you are available would also be helpful. Thank you!

You are still being concise and asking them to be the same in a gracious way while turning the focus to how they can help you help them. This message is far superior because the focus is on the caller!

"I will be in training all day but leave a message anyway."

To me the tone of this message says, I'm busy and maybe, if I can, I'll get back to you!" Saying "Leave a message anyway?" is the tip-off here.

Here's a better way:

"Hello, you've reached the office of Max Mazda in the HR department. Education is important so tell me what you need. I'll return your call by Friday. Bye!"

Another:

"This is Beverly Bonaville and I will return your call though it will not be today. If you need immediate assistance please press 246 for Emily now or I'll talk to you soon!"

These re-focused messages are all more effective because they:

- Lift the tone of the message to one that is more helpful and friendly;
- Make the caller feel good for calling;
- Give an action to take;
- Give only helpful information;
- Thank the caller.

Try Something Fun!

I'm a very casual and fun-loving person so I usually don't mind when someone leaves a message with a fun tone to it. Following are a few messages that I like because they make me smile:

- "Hi! It's Sue—At the beep you know what to do!" (short and snappy—and I *do* know what to do).
- "Hello, you've reached the office of Brad Bentley. Here comes the beep!" (upbeat, happy, short and to the point; I know who I've reached and I want to leave a message!")
- "Hello you've reached Shawna Schuh and I want to talk to you! I will too! Bye!"

> *"Wherever there is a human being,*
> *here is an opportunity for a kindness."*
> **Marcus Annaeus Seneca**

*   *   *   *   *

CHAPTER NINE REVIEW

1. **Don't answer if you can't serve the caller when the phone rings.**

2. **Don't blame or chastise your caller** for the past or expected future "sins" of others. Talking down to someone never builds him or her up!

3. **Don't tell the caller things they don't need to know** such as "I'm in meetings…" or "This is a busy time…"

4. **Focus on how you want the caller to feel.**

5. **Be upbeat and use a warm tone** in your voice and words.

6. **Give the caller actions to take.**

Chapter Ten

Leave Your Mark – Not a Stain!

---

*"You can't build up a reputation
on what you are going to do."*
Henry Ford

Leaving a Message – Rules to Leave a Mark!

So far, the focus in this book has been on what to say and how to say it in the message you leave for incoming calls. Now let's learn the rules to leave a mark on others voice mail so that you get better results when you call someone.

Rule #1: Say your phone number twice in the body of every message you leave when requesting a return call!

Say it once at the beginning of the message so the hearer can scribble it down, and then say it again before you finish so they can check what they scribbled and add any numbers they missed.

You would not believe the number of people who say to me, "I always leave my number twice." Then they call me and don't leave their number at all!

"Hello Bob, this is Shawna Schuh with Schuh Biz Productions at 503-662-3044. I'm returning your call about the Learn-A-Lot Project. I will be in the office after 3PM today and will try you then—or you can try to reach me at 503-662-3044. I look forward to speaking with you!"

Rule #2: Leave your number for your friends and family, too.

I travel a lot and when friends leave me a message while I'm away without leaving the number, I have to search around in my stuff to find it. Leaving it in the message saves me time and the hassle of hunting for it. Be nice to your friends; even with your best friends who you think have your number memorized. *It's still not about you; it's about them!* Leave your number and leave it again! Break the bad habit of not leaving your number—even when you call your mother. As people get older, they will appreciate your courtesy even more!

"Hi Julie, its Shawna at 503-662-3044. I miss you and want to hear about your trip! Call me when you can at 503-662-3044!"

Friends and family are the biggest offenders of not leaving numbers because love is not only blind sometimes its memory is poor!

Rule #3: Give em the full deal!

Full names identify you as a true professional and assist the other person who may need your full name when they return your call. This is especially true if you work in a large organization where there could be several people with the same first name as yours.

For example, I returned a call to Julie at XYZ Company after she left her number slowly in a pleasant tone of voice. When the phone rang, I was connected to the main receptionist, who asked me *which* Julie I was trying to reach. She hadn't left her last name, so I didn't have a clue. If she had left one of the following messages, I could have asked for the appropriate person rather than feeling at a loss for words with the receptionist:

This

"Hi, this is Julie with the XYZ Company."

OR

"Hi, this is Julie Brown in accounting with the XYZ Company."

Rule #4: Speak clearly.

When I taught finishing school we did a full three-hour session on voice. The reason was because using your voice well makes you a well rounded and understood professional. For voice mails it makes the listener happy lets you leave a good impression and fixes a lot of the needless problems people confront when they can not understand what you are saying. Clear concise messages are wonderful and people appreciate them!

Rule #5: Don't rush your message.

I love excitement, I love people, I love talking with people, and I talk fast! However, I love generating business even more and so I want to make it easy for people to do business with me. I consciously slow down my speaking speed when I leave a message so that they can receive, understand, and write down all pertinent information with ease.

Leaving an uplifting and informative message doesn't require speedy delivery. Just warming your voice with a smile will make your message more interesting. When you lift those lips, you won't rush and your message will sound warmer. If you think about the person who's receiving your message and speak to them as if they were in the room with you, your message will automatically sound warmer and more natural, rather than clipped or even curt.

Rule #6: Gruff isn't great.

If you live alone or don't have an opportunity to interact with other people in the morning to warm up your voice, your early morning phone calls may sound gruff or raspy. It's a smart idea to warm up your voice in order to do phone work or leave phone messages that convey warmth and excitement. So, if there's no one to talk to in the morning, talk to your pets, do a few vocal exercises, or sing along with the radio in the car during your commute to loosen up those chords and get rid of that gruff-sounding persona in your morning voice.

Rule #7: Keep your message short and sweet.

Long messages were the number one peeve in our survey. Then there's the issue of a rambling message with no number to call or one that you cannot understand. Rewinding and replaying one of these messages to get the number at the end is a real pain! Don't be inconsiderate. Keep your message short and sweet, including your full name and your number—twice. People will thank you for this professionalism!

> "Hi Al, this is Amber Albright returning your call. I'm at 503-662-3044. I look forward to speaking with you about the Martin project and my number again is 503-663-3044."

"Hi Susy, Matt Home here and I love your voice message! I can be reached at 503-662-3744 and I hope I can make your day like you made mine! It's Matt Home at 503-662-3044."

Rule #8: Return calls within 24 hours.

When someone goes out of their way to call you and leave a message, it's not only gracious but also professional to return their call within 24 hours.

At a recent event I met a woman who had met a friend of mine and then had tried to connect with her by phone. The first thing she said to me was, "Lisa never called me back!" Lisa's non-responsiveness had just put me on the spot, even though that wasn't her intention. What was I supposed to say to this woman? She was obviously confused as to why a professional and engaging person didn't have the courtesy to return her call in a timely manner.

Following this uncomfortable exchange, several things occurred to me.

- "Lisa" had lessened her impact and power by not returning this woman's call.

- The woman was upset, and depending on her level of self-esteem, may have turned it back on herself, as in "I'm not important enough to call back." Worse yet, she may have decided that Lisa thinks *she's* too important to return a call.

- Lisa's lack of phone courtesy is now in my knowledge base, so I'm concerned about her. It left me wondering about her breach of etiquette and it had put me in the uncomfortable position of defending her slight, which reflected on me personally and professionally.

All this upset because Lisa didn't return a call in a timely manner! Of course things happen and you may not be able to honor this rule at all times. When that's the case, have someone else return calls for you. Although this may not always endear you to your coworkers or staff, it is one way to keep a customer happy and protect your business image—the bases of return business.

If you do have someone do some of your return calls leave them a voice mail of thanks in off hours that they will get when they come in first thing the next morning. This is not only a gracious thing to do it will it will be appreciated and people in your office will continue to help you service your customers better!

I am always surprised when someone does not get back to me on the phone. Even when I've made a sales call, it's still gracious and good business to return the call, even if only to say, "I'm not interested; please don't call me again."

Rule #1: Say your phone number twice.

Rule #2: Leave your number for your friends and family, too.

Rule #3: Give em the Full Deal!

Rule #4: Speak clearly.

Rule #5: Don't rush your message.

Rule #6: Gruff isn't great.

Rule #7: Keep your message short and sweet.

Rule #8: Return calls within 24 hours.

What About Person-to-Person Messages?

The rules for leaving a message when you get someone other than the person you've called are pretty much identical to leaving a message on a voice-mail system. The only real difference is that you can thank the person for taking the message and say something nice to make their day too—hopefully ensuring that your message will be delivered accurately and in a timely fashion.

When I use the phone for business, I'd rather reach the voice mailbox of the person I'm calling and not the receptionist. When I get the receptionist I don't have the opportunity to use my voice and inflection to make a compelling personal impression on the person I'm trying to reach. So when I do get a receptionist I'll ask to be transferred to the voice mail of the person I'm trying to reach so I have more control on the impression and information I'm leaving.

Leaving a Message – When Not To

Sometimes it's far more professional to avoid leaving a message. For example, if you've just called to say "Hi" check in, it's OK to hang up without leaving a message. Using up voice mailbox space with unimportant messages that don't require a response is discourteous. Of course, you can leave a quick message like this:

"Hi, Joe, this Aubrey Smith, calling to check in. No need to return my call but you've been on my mind and I thought you'd like to know."

Here are some other times when it's better *not* to leave a message:

- **When you are in the middle of an emergency and the person you've called can't help you anyway because they're not there to talk to you in person.** I once received a frantic message from someone about some information they had to have that day. When I received the message it sent me into a tizzy because I didn't know if it was too late or what they needed and the distress in their tone was frantic. Don't be guilty of tormenting someone with a distressful message that they are obviously powerless to handle. If you must leave a message, include a time frame, i.e., "I absolutely must have the answer by noon" and state it as calmly and professionally as possible. If you can't abide by these rules, then *don't leave a message.*

- **You get a message that the person you are trying to reach is out of town or out of the office.** When I'm away, I really hate retrieving unimportant messages. I do appreciate receiving those that are important to what I am doing or that require action that I can take. If what you're calling about doesn't require a response or immediate action and the person you called was considerate enough to let you know that they're away, don't fill up their system with trivia. Instead, make a note to yourself to call them when they return. Of course, if you are getting back to a client to tell them that you have completed something that will ease their mind, leave a short message to that effect—that's about making them feel good, the key goal for voice mail.

- **You are not prepared to leave a good message.** It would be better to hang up and call back when you have the information you need to leave a meaningful message. There's a person I know that leaves messages with so many "ands" and "ums" you feel uncomfortable listening to him. It would be better for this person to get clear about what they need before they leave a message.

Ten Tips for Leaving Effective Messages

Learn to use your phone time wisely and leave messages for others during off-hours. This can save time and avoid unnecessary and time-consuming phone conversations.

So call people and leave a message to:

1. Inform a potential client/customer about your products or services.

2. Leave requested information, such as product specifications or availability.

3. Confirm that an order or service is in the works or has been sent.

4. Confirm an appointment (used as a reminder).

5. Share new product information.

6. Leave a project update with a client.

7. Show concern or support when warranted.

8. Stay connected with someone important to you or your business without getting involved in a long conversation.

9. Return that salesperson's call and tell him or her that you are not interested in doing business with them, or that you are not interested in their service or product at this time. (You'll get another call down the road with this last one.)

10. Make someone's day!

Using voice mail for any of the above reasons during off hours is courteous because it doesn't interrupt someone with worthy but non-essential information during productive work hours. There's another bonus. The person you called will probably get your message first thing in the morning when they pick up their messages and you'll get a call-back when they're alert and fresh.

*   *   *   *   *

Chapter Ten Review

1. **Get your attitude right** before you call anyone.

2. **Review the 8 rules for leaving your mark.**

3. **Know when NOT to leave a message.**

4. **If you get a "live" person you can ask to be transferred to voice mail**

5. **Know your goal when leaving a message for someone.**

6. **You leave a mark when you leave a great message!**

Chapter Eleven

Just Because You Can, Doesn't Mean You Should!

"Ninety per cent of the art of living consists of getting on with people one cannot stand."
Samuel Goldwyn

Voice Mail Is Here to Stay

There once was a man named Louie who began experiencing an irritating problem. By 9:00 AM each morning, his ears began ringing and his eyeballs popped out. Well Louie was under a lot of job stress so his supervisor suggested that he see a psychologist.

"It's your job." The psychologist said. "Quit your job, find a new line of work and your problem will be solved." So Louie who hated that his ears were ringing and his eyeballs popped out, quit his job.

After only one day his ears stated ringing again, and his eyeballs popped out. So he went to the doctor who suggested the source of his problem was his teeth. So Louie arranged to have all his teeth pulled but that didn't work either. His ears still rang and his eyeballs continued to pop. Now Louie is really frustrated so he goes to see a specialist who worked primarily with ringing ears and popping eyeballs. Louie endured a week of intense testing and then the specialist said, "I'm sorry but you only have three month to live."

Louie was so upset! "I've quit my job, had all my teeth removed and now I find out I'm going to die." But what could Louie do? He decided to enjoy his final three months. He sold his house and withdrew all of his life's savings. Louie went on a shopping spree and bought a sports car, a boat and even decided to have his suits tailored.

The tailor was meticulous in taking Louie's measurements, "That will be a 34 sleeve," the tailor determined, "and, let's see, a 16-inch neck."

"No, no," Louie stopped him, "I've always worn a 15-inch neck. Make my collars size 15."

"Whatever you say," replied the tailor. "But I'll tell you one thing; if you keep wearing size 15 collars, your ears will ring and your eyeballs will begin popping out."

Poor Louie caused all his own problems because he didn't realize that one little adjustment could make such a big difference! The title of this chapter is "Just because you can doesn't mean you should!" and I think Louie is a prime example of how easy it is to get caught up in doing things the way we've always done them which isn't always the best way.

I found that story of Louie in a great book called, *Words for all Occasions* compiled by Glenn Van Ekedren and it's one of the sources I use for some of the quotes I include in my voice mail messages. I don't always include quotes and as I've worked on this book I find myself including less and less because once again, just because I can doesn't always mean that I should! The input I received on this book helped me do a lot of streamlining and though I still try to do the "extra" and incorporate all the techniques I've given you, I'm finding myself getting cleaner and quicker on my messages because so many people want them that way. My goal is to always make the caller feel valued and good but it's also to use my messages to the best advantage. The following information will be somewhat of a review, some new slants on what we have already covered and will clarify using voice mail as a business tool as well as giving you perceptions from respondents of our survey.

> *"I am an optimist. It does not seem*
> *too much use being anything else."*
> **Sir Winston Churchill**

While I was writing this book, I polled a lot of people about voice mail, including readers of my every-once-in-awhile ezine, "Schuh Polish" (go to www.BusinessGraces.com). One of the questions I asked was, "What irritates you most about voice mail?"

I got many intense replies so I am more convinced than ever that most of the world isn't using voice mail as the vital business-building tool it can be. Here are a few of the responses that came through loud and clear.

Voice messages that are too long

This irritant won the poll, hands down.

> *"Time is the most valuable thing a man can spend."*
> **Theophrastus**

Here's a good example of a bad (read that too long) message:

"Hi you've reached the office of Oliver Oldsmobile with the Total Control Company and I'm sorry there is no one to answer your call. If you want to reach the accounting department please press 1. If you want to leave a personal message for me, press 2. To reach my assistant, Harry, press 3. Or you can call directly at 888-888-8888, or you could try me on my mobile phone at 777-777-7777. Otherwise, just leave your name, phone number, and a message at the tone and I will get back to you as soon as I can. Thank you and have a great day!"

Not only is this message way too long, it also includes way too much information for anyone listening to absorb or write down—without listening to it again and again.

The moral? **Be brief.** The minimal message should include the following things—all in a positive tone:

- Your name
- Your organization
- A promise

This is true whether you're leaving a message on your system for your callers or leaving a message on someone else's voice mail, requesting action from them. Going on and on in a message is confusing and a waste of time—yours and the listener's. *Don't do it!*

To be effective on messages you leave on others voice mail include the following in your message to them:

- Your full name
- The number where you can be reached
- The reason for your call
- Your number a second time
- A closing that asks for appropriate action on the part of the recipient

Here are a few examples of a request for action:

- "Would you please call me back with the model number and color you would like to order?"
- "It would help us both if you would tell me the date you had in mind."
- "I'll get right back to you as soon as you confirm the price. You can leave that on my voice mail if you miss me."

Don't give the listener a lot of options. When someone calls, they usually want immediate help or satisfaction.

Define yourself

If the name of your company or service doesn't clearly identify what you do, there is one more piece of information to include in your message. When I get a message from Dick's Dog Wash, I know exactly who called, but if you say you're from the Spokes company and I've never heard of it, I don't know who you are or what you're about. So, if you don't have a defining name to leave in your message, *include a short defining statement.*

A defining statement is a short sentence that tells the caller or the listener what it is you do. Sometimes simply identifying the department the caller has reached will be enough. Here's an example of a brief, defining statement:

"Hello you've reached Jane Suzuki with the Suzuki Institute where we do consulting work with the health care industry. I would love to help you and will return your call. Thank you for calling the Suzuki Institute. We believe in the power of healing!"

This is short and simple and I know exactly whom I've reached, what her company does, and a little about the company philosophy. Notice that this is a statement, not a sales message. It's just pertinent information with a hint of the personality of Jane's business.

> If necessary, include a defining statement in your message—a sentence that states what you do and its benefit to the caller.

Will a defining statement help the caller? Only if it clarifies for them who they have reached and how it can help them. In the above example I now know that Jane Suzuki is involved in the health care industry and if that isn't who I need I can save us both time by moving on to someone who can help me more.

A defining statement is also a great asset for you professionally. I belong to the National Speakers Association and most professionals in this industry try to help people by giving their defining statement when meeting someone for the first time because saying you are a professional or motivational speaker is way to broad.

Example of poor response:
"I'm a motivational speaker"

Better response:
"I work with people focused organizations who want more profitable relationships"

For others in the service industry it can have the same benefit. Example for a CPA

Example of poor response:
"I'm a CPA"

Better response:
"I work with entrepreneurs who want to keep more of what they make."

This last example makes me want to learn more about this person's business because the benefit to me could be immense. Meeting someone who gives me their title is more about them. See how all these things tie in together?

Focus on the needs of callers and customers and you will get better results.

Getting messages that include fax numbers

Survey respondents said this is another irritating thing about voice messages. Most people don't need your fax number. Including it is unnecessary and can cause confusion when someone is trying to write down the pertinent information they need. If they want your fax number, the caller will ask for it in the message they leave for you.

Overselling in a message

Just because you can do a sales pitch on your voice mail doesn't mean you should! Listeners mentioned many times that they dislike getting a heavy-duty sales pitch in the context of a voice message. If you call a company to discuss their product or service, the sale is already partially made simply because you called their number. Self-serving, blatant sales messages like the one that follows are generally not appreciated. They're usually too long, too.

"Hello, you've reached the Roof Top Company where we have provided first-rate customer service for over thirty years to a wide range of clients. We'd love to help you as well, so leave your name and number at the sound of the tone and one of our experienced sales professionals will return your call! Thank you for calling Roof Top Company and have a top-of-the-roof day!"

How could it be better? Make it shorter and direct it to the customer's needs—like this perhaps:

"Hello, you've reached the Roof Top Company and we'd love to help you with all your roofing needs! We will return your call within 24 hours. Thanks for calling. Have a top-of-the-roof day!"

This message leaves a better impression because:

- The caller knows immediately that they dialed the right number—if they are interested in roofing;
- The caller knows this company wants to help them;
- The company promises a call-back in a certain time frame;
- The company has some personality!

This example also reinforces the concept of a defining statement. Here are two more:

- "Hello, You've reached the Cookie Company and we're cooking up good things for you!"
- "Hi! You've reached Bob's Barber Shop where we're waiting to give you the cutting edge!"

If you want your callers to take actions
include a call to action in your messeages.

Individuals can use defining statements to focus on the caller in their voice messages too. For example:

- "Hi! This is Norma in Accounting and I have the numbers you're looking for!"

- "Hello you've reached the voice mail of Al with Excite Productions where we're excited to work with you!"

* * * * *

Chapter Eleven Review

1. **Little things can help or hurt you.** Be aware that the problem could be that you've been doing something one way for so long you've lost sight of what the challenges are like Louie.

2. **Avoid leaving a long message.** Include things in your message that benefit the person on the other end and be quick about it!

3. **A one-sentence defining statement** can be a great benefit to add to your message if it helps your caller.

4. **Think more about serving your caller than of making the "sale" with your message.** The sales will come.

5. **Think about how you want the caller to feel.**

Chapter Twelve

Productivity Tools

---

*"Calm self-confidence is as
far from conceit as the desire to earn a
decent living is remote from greed."*
Channing Pollock

A Brief Review

To become highly effective when using voice mail, it is essential to think about this electronic medium in efficient and creative ways that will direct even more business and success your way.

It's also essential to review the lessons you've learned thus far. In every thing you do, ***put people first.*** Even if you never speak to someone in person, you can still accomplish your business goals by using your image and tone to leave the impression that you care about the person on the other end of the line. (Of course you must really care about the person on the other end of the line not just give the impression you do.) Leaving concise and engaging messages is another part of the equation as well as focusing on how you can best serve the person you've called or the one who has called you.

I've accomplished a lot of productive business by leaving and receiving messages. I don't need to hear a live voice to find out that I just got the speaking engagement. A phone message can do the job, too. As a matter of fact, I like to get the good news on voice mail so I can play it back several times and re-experience the joy without having to act professional when I get an in-person call with the news. Why, I've even been known to do a little jig during a phone message that contains great news!

The remainder of this final chapter focuses on a few techniques that can help you develop more effective voice-mail habits. Make sure that you have implemented all the other voice mail rules set forth in previous chapters including:

- Understand the philosophy behind the voice.

- Tune up your tone of voice.

- Make sure every message you leave focuses on the caller/ customer.

- Keep messages short and to the point.

- Use language and content that works best for you and your business.

When you are confident that your voice messages meet these criteria, try adding some of these productivity tools to your arsenal and you will really know *How to Nail Voice Mail.*

Four Tips for Leaving Tip-top Messages

Whenever you leave a message, always use the 4-S system:

1. **Stand up to speak.** Do this when recording your own voice-mail message and when you are leaving a message for someone else. Standing up puts your breath in a different place and gives you more control of your voice. Most people tend to slouch when they sit but for the short time that you are recording a message, stand up. It will make a big difference in your tone.

2. **Smile.** We've already reviewed this but it's vital so I'm repeating it. If you really want to be effective on voice mail, smile while recording your messages!

3. **Say who you are in every message you leave.** Simply launching into a conversation or message is less effective. Don't expect that the other person will automatically recognize your voice. It can be a put off. Be completely professional on voice mail and you'll always make a great impression, leaving no doubt that you are the one who deserves the business!

4. **State the reason for your call,** even if it's as simple as "I just wanted to let you know you were on my mind." Many survey respondents disliked messages like this: "Hi, this is Jim. Call me!" Although this message might seem direct and to the point, it's also curt, demanding, and lacking in warmth or concern for the other person. Poor Jim may never get a callback and wonder why.

> **The four S's:**
> **STAND up**
> **SMILE**
> **SAY who you are**
> **STATE the reason**

Learn to Use Business Voice Mail Systems Effectively

If you don't know how to take full advantage of the system your company has installed, pull out the instruction manual for a quick review.

Forward, please

Learn to use the system to forward voice mail and you will save yourself a lot of time while improving your efficiency and effectiveness.

If someone leaves you a voice message but you know that Sally in the Customer Service department is the person who can offer the best service to the caller, use your system to forward the message. That will save you time and likely get the caller a better response. Be sure to alert Sally that you are forwarding the message because you think she is more experienced or capable of handling the call. She'll appreciate the "heads-up" and the compliment and the caller will be better served.

Use the broadcast option

There is also a feature on some message systems that allows a person to send voice mail out to a group. You design who is on your list and you record a message that goes to everyone. Imagine the possibilities with this feature! You can use it to improve group communications and keep up company morale by keeping everyone who should be in the loop informed at the same time. Gossip and hurt feelings will be minimized if you use this option effectively. Use it to get out information that can help everyone succeed at meeting established goals. Here are a few things you can broadcast:

- Announcements of upcoming meetings. A voice message is more personal than e-mail. Of course, you can follow up the broadcast message with a group e-mail including more information and the meeting agenda.

- Bad or sad news—before it becomes a rumor. Squelching gossip is easy when everyone gets the word at the same time.

- Client acquisitions—a win for everyone!

- Goals that have been met.

- New goals.

- Pricing changes.

- Recognition; send out a voice mail to everyone when someone does extraordinary work. The praise will go farther and carry more weight. Everyone loves recognition for a job well done.

- Reminders about inspections or insurance renewals or annual events.

- Thought for the day—to build enthusiasm or provoke thought.

- Year-end information.

Review What You've Said

If the message system—yours or the person's you've called—gives you the option to review your message, be sure to do it! It's like using spell check in e-mail. Yes, it takes a little extra time but it gives you the security of knowing that your message went out without obvious errors or omissions.

The other bonus? The more you review what you say and how you say it on messages that you leave, the better you get at refining your tone and content for the best possible response.

Help People Help You

My customers are the focus and most of them become my friends so it's fun to leave them happy or encouraging messages and I love it when they do that for me too. If you've ever gotten a great voice mail message you know how wonderful if is to keep the message to review later, forward it to the team that helped you with the success, or act on information at your convenience. Here are a few messages that help people help you:

- "Please call me anytime with that information."
- "I check messages often and would like to hear a message from you!"
- "I love voice mail so please leave me a message."

Giving your callers permission to leave you a message actually makes it easier for them to leave you a good one.

Prioritize Your Calls

Make it a habit to prioritize your messages as you receive them. Here's how I prioritize mine. Use it or adapt it to suit your purposes.

1. Act-now calls
2. Business-hours-only calls
3. After-hours calls

Act-now calls

Answer these calls as soon as possible but only when you are fully available to give the caller your undivided attention. I make it point to check voice mail often during the day and I let my callers know that. It's easy to miss calls when you are on the phone serving someone else, especially if you don't pick up the phone again that day and don't hear the tone that indicates you have a message waiting. Giving prompt service is a hallmark of my business and it works.

Business-hours-only calls

You can schedule phone time into your notebook or Palm Pilot right alongside each message for calls that must be handled during business hours. Perhaps you need to call back to re-schedule an appointment or talk to a retail sales clerk about a pending purchase. I prefer to call a doctor's or dentist's office in off hours and specify when I would like an appointment, then let them call me back to confirm the date and time or give me additional options. Sometimes, however, that won't work so I must make the call during regular business hours. I've made it a habit to make a list of the calls I need to make in my notebook every day so nothing falls through the cracks and my productivity remains at a high level.

After-hours call-backs

I love handling voice mail after hours because I can make these calls anytime and anywhere I happen to be at the time. With my notes and numbers handy (on my Palm Pilot), I can make calls while sitting in an airport or from a hotel room in a different time zone without distractions. I also do these calls from home late at night or very early in the morning when the house is quiet.

After hours call backs work well also because I live on the West Coast. For example, I returned a call at 5:30 AM, which was 8:30 AM on the East Coast. I actually reached the person I was calling, rather than voice mail this time. They were surprised but pleased to get the early-bird call and we completed our business efficiently and effectively because we were both fresh. Then I had time in my day to go work out with a clear sense that I had already accomplished some key work for the day. Yes, I have a life but it works around me rather than vice versa. That's the best thing about learning to nail voice mail—it allows me to design my work and personal life to my advantage!

Three Key Concepts for Better Communication

I want to leave you with three key concepts that will help you improve the effectiveness of all of your business communications. Use them faithfully and you are sure to make more effective and efficient use of your phone and the vital, business-building potential of voice mail. You can "nail voice mail!"

1. **Schedule time to do the work.**

   Whether it's voice mail or e-mail or working on a current project, having things scheduled makes you more professional, more organized, and more effective.

2. **Be prepared (aka, organized).**

   When you have key information at your fingertips and can answer the caller's questions more effectively. You will also prosper and build better relationships because of the positive, professional impression you make.

3. **Keep a record.**

   Keeping track of what you've done and have yet to do makes it easier to improve your performance and service and complete customer follow-up in a timely and profitable fashion. I keep a notebook by the phone and my Palm Pilot so I know whom I'm calling and what I'm doing. Most of my business transactions happen over the phone so it's a vital and essential tool.

   *   *   *   *   *

CHAPTER TWELVE REVIEW

1. **Use the 4-S System:** Stand, Smile, Say who you are, and State the reason in every message you leave.

2. **Forward messages whenever appropriate** to best meet the needs of the caller.

3. **Use the broadcast option** to reach many people at once with the same message.

4. **Review the message you've just recorded** to make sure it says what you want and sounds the way you want it to sound. Re-do it until you are happy with it in every way.

5. **Help people help you by encouraging them to use voice mail** to get their needs and yours met effectively and efficiently.

6. **Prioritize your time and call-backs** for the most effective use of phone time.

"Love begins when a person feels another person's need to be as important as his own."

Harry Stack Sullivan

"Do all the good you can
By all the means you can
In all the ways you can
In all the places you can
At all the times you can
To all the people you can
As long as ever you can!"

John Wesley

Thank you for reading this book and blessings to you!

Appendix

The A through Z's of Effective Voice Mail

Here's some reminders of everything you've learned about using voice mail effectively and efficiently for personal and professional profit. Of course there's an extra or two in there because—well—you know me!

- Add a little love to your messages!
- Ask yourself, "How do I want my caller to feel?"
- Be brief.
- Call people back.
- Do warm up your voice.
- Energize your caller.
- Focus on the caller.
- Give your phone number twice.
- Have fun.
- Include a little "extra" in your message.
- Joy can be felt over the phone.
- Keep your message current.
- Leave a great impression.
- Make someone's day.
- Nice works!
- Offer assistance and encouragement.
- Promise only what you *can and will* deliver.
- Quotes are great "extras."
- Record a new message daily, if appropriate.
- Review and revise your message before you leave it.
- Say your full name.
- Set a positive, upbeat, happy tone.
- Speak slowly and distinctly.

- Smile.
- Stand up when you are leaving a message.
- State the reason for your call.
- Think of the caller first.
- Use voice mail as an effective and efficient business tool.
- Voice mail is easy to nail!
- Warm it up!
- Xtra add what you need for Extraordinary!
- You have the power to do more!
- Zest for doing the best guarantees positive results!

And, just as a final reminder, here are a few voice mail "don'ts" that bear repeating:

Don't:

- Apologize.
- Bore the listener.
- Chastise your callers.
- Forget to leave your number.
- Get too cute.
- Leave more information than the caller needs or wants to hear.
- Mumble.
- Neglect to return a call.
- Rush your message.
- State the obvious.
- Talk too fast.
- Use a monotone voice.

"You don't get to choose
how you're going to die. Or when.
You can only decide how you're going to live."

Joan Baez

About the Author

Shawna Schuh is a business humorist and people performance specialist. She has over twenty years of experience in teaching communications, human relations, and all forms of business and personal etiquette. Raised and still living in rural Oregon, Shawna has taught every age group from fourteen-year-old aspiring models with raging hormones to university students, to corporate CEOs (Also with raging hormones). Her information has withstood the test of time and works for anyone interested in improving their interactions with others.

In addition to *How to Nail Voice Mail*, Shawna is the author of *51 Ways To Pick Up Your Get Up & Go!* and the e-book, *How to Out Finesse the Competition*. She has also written five educational booklets on social graces. She is the creator and constant contributor to www.BusinessGraces.com, a website that addresses all forms of business and social etiquette. She has also performed in over 150 television and radio commercials and seven films. Shawna has worked with people from all walks of life, including casino owners, builders and contractors, hair replacement companies, and CEOs of major companies. She has been there done that—sometimes twice!

Join the graciousness circle and continue to get
great cutting edge information from Shawna!

Visit: www.BusinessGraces.com and sign up for
the Free Every-once-in-awhile ezine, *Schuh Polish*.

To bring Shawna's unique blend of business skills and
humor to your organization call Sandy McCready at:
877-377-1946

To contact Shawna directly:
503-662-3044
or
Shawna@BusinessGraces.com

Volume Discounts

Because we know that *How To Nail Voice Mail* is an important resource for any organization and for *everyone* who answers or uses a phone, we want to help you make it available to everyone on your team. You can purchase this book in volume at a discount so that you can make sure every team member is at their absolute best when they leave a message on theirs or anyone's voice-mail system.

We offer hefty discounts when you purchase large quantities. In addition, we'll be happy to customize the books in large-volume orders with your company's logo. We'll even add a message from your leader inside the book if you like.

How to Nail Voice Mail is a great gift for meeting or conference attendees and it's also a wonderful reward to help everyone celebrate a stellar quarter or other special business accomplishment. Give it as a gift and get one in return—even greater performance!

For more information on pricing and customization for *How to Nail Voice Mail,* call our office at 877-474-2962.

Order Form

Boost Your Business…with a gift of
How to Nail Voice Mail
by Shawna Schuh

Please send me _____ copies of *How to Nail Voice Mail* at \$14.95 each, plus \$3.00 shipping per book.

I'm sending a check along with this order for \$ _____

MAKE CHECKS PAYABLE TO:
Shawna Schuh
Schuh Biz Publications
24241 Hwy. 47
Gaston, Oregon 97119
Phone: 503-662-3044 • Fax: 503-662-4381
E-mail: Shawna@BusinessGraces.com

PLEASE CHARGE MY:

VISA# _____ Exp. Date _____

MasterCard# _____ Exp. Date _____

Signature: _____
(for credit card orders only)

E-mail address: _____

Or, make your purchase online at our secure website:
www.BusinessGraces.com

SHIPPING INFORMATION:

Name: _____

Organization: _____

Address: _____

City / State / Zip: _____

Phone: _____ Fax: _____